THE REALITY OF PROBATION

The Reality of Probation

A formal ethnography of process and practice

JASON DITTON
Criminology Research Unit
Sociology Department
Glasgow University

ROSLYN FORD
Department of Social Policy & Social Work
Glasgow University

Avebury

Aldershot · Brookfield USA · Hong Kong · Singapore · Sydney

Published by
Avebury
Ashgate Publishing Limited
Gower House
Croft Road
Aldershot
Hants GU11 3HR
England

Ashgate Publishing Company
Old Post Road
Brookfield
Vermont 05036
USA

British Library Cataloguing in Publication Data

Ditton, Jason
    Reality of Probation: Formal Ethnography of
    Process and Practice
    I. Title II. Ford, Roslyn
    364.63
ISBN 1 85628 858 7

Library of Congress Cataloging-in-Publication Data

Ditton, Jason
    The reality of probation: a formal ethnography of
    process and practice / Jason Ditton and Roslyn Ford.
        p.   cm.
    Includes bibliographical references.
    ISBN 1-85628-858-7: $55.95 (est)
    1. Probation--Scotland. 2. Sheriffs--Scotland--Attitudes.
    3. Social workers--Scotland--Attitudes. 4. Social work
    with criminals--Scotland. I. Ford, Roslyn. II. Title.
    HV9347.A5D58 1994   94-18855
    364.6'3'09411--dc20   CIP

Typeset by
Samuel Phillips
12 Kew Terrace
Glasgow G12 0TE
Printed and Bound in Great Britain by
Athenaeum Press Ltd, Newcastle upon Tyne.

Contents

Contents

Acknowledgements

We have talked to so many people that we cannot adequately relay our thanks by listing everybody by name. Our key sources - the probationers, the supervising officers and the sheriffs - must all remain anonymous, although they deserve our greatest appreciation.

The original research was funded by the Scottish Office Home and Health Department, and directed jointly by Jason Ditton and Roslyn Ford.

Roslyn Ford and Ann Laybourn undertook all the fieldwork, and Barbara Perry assisted when the pressure of work was simply too much. Roslyn Ford and Ann Laybourn were chiefly responsible also for analysing the data, and for preparing the various reports on which this book draws heavily.

The team was fortunate enough also to be continuously assisted by Mary Snaddon. Her contribution was far in excess of the level usual for a part-time administrator, and without it this research would not have been concluded at all.

1 Introduction

1.1 Context

Probation is a method of dealing with specially selected offenders which consists of the conditional suspension of punishment while the offender is placed under personal supervision and is given individual guidance and treatment (United Nations, 1951, p. 16).

'Punishment in the community' is highly topical yet hardly new. Probation was first introduced as a disposal in 1907 under the Probation of Offenders Act, when it became available for any offender, except where the offence carried a sentence fixed by law, and provided the offender himself agreed to submit to the order. The subsequent development of the system depended on the availability of a body of people to undertake the supervision which was largely carried out in the early days by police court missionaries. These were attached to various religious organisations and were already engaged in evangelical work in the large cities with many of those who appeared before the magistrates' courts. In addition the 1907 Act provided for the appointment of probation officers, marking the first step towards a full time salaried social work service.

Since that time probation has remained as the major social work service to the courts, although the legislative framework has been developed and modified over the years. The essential aims and purpose of probation were reiterated in the Criminal Justice (Scotland) Act 1949, but in the 1966 White Paper, *Social Work and the Community*, plans for placing it within 'comprehensive' Social Work departments were suggested. These suggestions were implemented in the Social Work (Scotland) Act 1968, which, together with the Criminal Procedure (Scotland) Act 1975, forms the current legislative framework for probation in Scotland.

Probation began with, and retains, the structural ambivalence clearly brought out in the above definition by the United Nations. It has elements of control in that the original offence remains punishable throughout the period of probation if the offender either commits a further offence or violates the conditions of the probation order. At the same time however, it has an operational basis which focuses on the treatment of specially selected offenders rather than the punishment of any particular offence. The elements of personal supervision involving individual guidance and treatment further suggest rehabilitation rather than punishment.

As we move towards the millennium and ominously close to the centenary of British probation, it is the current management of this structural ambivalence by those involved in probation in Scotland which this book seeks to reveal.

1.2 Sheriffs

1.2.1 Previous studies

The Scottish experience in this area is not well documented, although one study carried out in 1978 provides some insight into sheriffs' attitudes towards probation and how these influence sentencing practices (Scottish Office, 1982). In-depth interviews with twelve sheriffs showed there was no general agreement about the kind of situations where probation was or was not a suitable disposal and they found it difficult to explain their ways of operating when faced with individual decisions. Each seemed to follow idiosyncratic guidelines coupled with rules of thumb which together provided a ready frame of reference for the case in hand. As one sheriff explained when discussing the identification of suitable offenders, 'you know them when you see them but its difficult to put it over to you as following a system'.

Nevertheless a number of different general views of probation emerged. One sheriff saw it as a let-off and another as unsuitable for serious offenders as they deserved a more obvious punishment. A third regarded it as inappropriate for petty offenders, as they were often too inadequate for social workers to deal with, and a fourth as too lenient for first offenders where a sharper deterrent was required to 'nip things in the bud'.

Sheriffs did agree however that they were more likely to use probation for female offenders, regarding them as more 'appropriate' subjects. They thought, for example, that women often offended out of desperation and needed someone to help them sort out their problems, or that they were dependent on a male who was the real problem.

This study suggests that judicial eclecticism might stem partly from the structural ambivalence of probation. It was certainly true that, when considering probation as a disposal, sheriffs were influenced by their perception of the quality and efficacy of supervision provided by their local Social Work Department. However what was considered an effective service was unclear. There was little knowledge of what the probation relationship and process entailed; views on frequency of contact varied considerably and, beyond emphasising practical help, sheriffs were reluctant to interfere with the social work process or the discretion of supervising social workers.

1.2.2 This study

Previous work seemed to show that, in general, Sheriffs adopted one of three main approaches to probation as a disposal. There were those who limited their use of probation because they regarded social work resources as inadequate; a second group were favourably disposed towards probation, but wished to see a greater disciplinary element and more innovatory methods of supervision; and finally there were those who viewed probation as mainly suitable for treating, in the words of one sheriff, 'sort of mental cases'.

Although many of today's sheriffs have been appointed since the introduction of generic social work departments, it may well be that some of their views reflected past experience of specialist probation supervision prior to the passage of the 1968 Act. Certainly before then the collective judicial view was tightly focused on the offence and on preventing reoccurrence. Consider the following statement from a memo submitted by the Sheriffs' Substitute Association in response to the 1966 White Paper. It unequivocally adopts a 'control' line:

> the essential reason for the probation officer's intervention in the affairs of any individual is that he has been found guilty by the court of an offence against the criminal law and not that he is the victim of some deprivation or handicap. The probation officer's main duty, whether in supervision or assessment, is to try to ensure that this individual will not offend against the criminal law again.

The White Paper itself took a more 'care' orientation:

> the main duty of the probation officer - personal social work with the offender and his family in the community - is basically similar to that of other social workers.

This orientation, implemented in the genericism of the 1968 Act, while emphasising different and broader priorities for probation supervision, left the legal meaning and practice of probation untouched. Thus doubts and uncertainties were created about the appropriateness of probation disposals, the role and function of supervising social workers, and the differing and sometimes conflicting expectations of probation supervision and probationer behaviour.

In order to explore these and other areas of concern, interviews were carried out with twenty three sheriffs in four courts in different areas of Scotland. A number of those interviewed had experience of more than one court and were thus in a position to make useful comparisons about differences between organisation and practice in different geographical and administrative areas. A structured schedule was used as the basis for in-depth, open ended interviews, which were tape recorded on all but one occasion. During interview, sheriffs were encouraged to introduce and discuss issues which they themselves thought important.

1.3 Probationers

1.3.1 Previous studies

A number of studies emphasising environmental issues have investigated the backgrounds of probationers and produced cogent arguments for the significance of certain environmental variables in terms of perceptions and expectations of probation and in relation to its likely outcome and effectiveness (Davies 1969 and 1974, Davies and Sinclair 1971). There was for example, strong evidence that the father-son relationship was crucial for young adult male probationers, and was closely linked to their chances of success in probation. While subsequent findings from a probation hostel population drew similar conclusions about the warden-probationer relationship, both studies concluded that the mother-son and matron-probationer relationship was not significant in terms of probation failure or success.

Other findings indicated that, in the cases studied, neither material difficulties in themselves, nor unwillingness to discuss problems appeared to precipitate further offences, and that only a small proportion of probationers appeared to resent the authority structure. Furthermore, the favourable and steadying influence that marriage is thought to have on the behaviour of offenders (if we go by the contents of many social enquiry reports) seems to be something of a delusion. In the majority of cases marriage only added to the existing problems.

To gain a better understanding of environmental factors which affect success in probation, Davies analysed empirical data on a sample of 507 seventeen to twenty year old probationers and identified three theoretically and practically relevant areas: the level of family support available; the relationship between the individual and his work; and the level of 'crime contamination' (Davies 1973). Broadly speaking, if probationers did badly in any of these areas they fared poorly overall.

The relationship between an individual and his environment can be conceptualised at different levels of complexity, each of which has implications for probation supervision. At the first level a cause and effect model is assumed, in which the individual is entirely at the mercy of external stresses and responds to them in an *ad hoc* way. The second level emphasises the interaction of stress factors in the environment, while the third recognises that, in addition to the interacting factors, further counteracting influences may militate against the resolution of identified problems (Emery and Trist, 1969). At the most complex level a picture of confused perplexity is presented:

> It is as if the ground - or society itself - were in motion, so that...larger and potentially unreachable variables have to be taken into account - for example, economic difficulties in the immediate area giving a high unemployment rate, political policies determining regional prosperity, urban decay and lack of play space in city centres which may have particular relevance for offence behaviour, and the social class and educational background of the individual determining his life aspirations and, contrarily, the likelihood of his being able to satisfy them within his environmental context (Davies, 1974, p. 6).

1.3.2 This study

Following an analysis of national statistics for several years immediately prior to commencing this study, we selected four courts which showed varying trends in the use of probation over that period. From these courts we then selected 86 recent probation cases which formed the organisational basis of the study. We interviewed sheriffs in the courts where the orders were made and we interviewed the social workers who supervised the orders. Although quantitative data was collected and analysed, we were more concerned to examine the definitions of and perspectives on probation and to explore the motives, attitudes, emotions and experience surrounding it, than to search for significant correlations between factors, persons or groups.

The length of the probation order was the principal criterion in the selection of probationers, with the selected cases in each of the four length categories proportionately matching, as far as possible, the numbers given probation in

Sheriff Courts in Scotland in 1985, the most recent full year for which data was then available. We also obtained as wide a range of offenders as possible in terms of gender, age and type of offence. Just over half of the orders were for a year, 21 for 2 years, 7 for three years and 6 for 18 months. There were 59 men and 27 women, whose ages ranged from the late teens to the early sixties, with 34 under 21 years of age, 35 in their twenties and the remaining ten over 30. They had been placed on probation for a wide variety of offences: 41 for charges of theft (often associated with housebreaking); 16 for assault; 11 for breach of the peace, and 7 for sex offences. A further 21 charges included fraud, fire raising, drug offences, road traffic offences and offences against the Children and young Persons' Acts. As the numbers indicate many were given probation for several offences.

The aim of interviews with probationers was to explore their perception and understanding of probation, both in terms of its legal definition and the process itself. We asked them about their initial expectations of supervision and the demands they thought it would make upon them. With probationers who were some way into their period of supervision, we sought to identify any discrepancies between those expectations and what had actually been achieved. We tried to discover how they felt about being on probation. Was it seen as a stigmatising process; as being 'let off' or, indeed, as some kind of status symbol? What kinds of definitions underlay these differing perceptions? We also tried to obtain their views about the quality of service they were getting and whether, from their point of view, being on probation had anything to offer.

1.4 Social workers

We interviewed social workers with much the same agenda in mind, but this time looking at the issues from the other side of supervision. What did social workers understand by probation supervision? Were concepts like treatment, help, advice, guidance and assistance the notions which underpinned their practice, and if so, was there a relationship between general ideology and work with individual cases? What kind of criteria were used to modify general ideologies according to specific situations? Other areas of interest related to the aims of supervision as seen by the supervisor, both in general and specific terms. Did they, for example, draw up or even have in mind a plan of action for each probationer? Were there limits to the kind of support they felt able to give and, if so, how were these limits defined? Was there a practical dilemma between care and control and again, if so, how was this dealt with? How far too did the supervisory response depend on the social worker's interpretation of the offence as opposed to its legal definition?

The 60 social workers we interviewed varied considerably in background and work experience. Six came from a specialist background of work with offenders, either from the former probation service or from work in prisons, list D establishments or specialist teams. Some 47 had a generic background, 17 of whom had less than three years experience. Three workers were unqualified social work assistants, one was a social work student and three were senior social workers not directly holding cases, but supervising social workers who were. None of those interviewed had specialist offender posts and none were currently working in specialist offender teams. Ten however expressed a special interest in this area of work and some of these had weighted case loads, carrying a greater proportion of probation cases than their colleagues. Supervision of the probationers was therefore carried out almost entirely by social workers with general training and experience, carrying a full range of social work duties in addition to their probation cases.

The 86 probationers who were the focus of the research were followed through during the two year research period, using in-depth interviews and detailed analysis of cases notes. All supervising social workers were interviewed at least once and often on several occasions and, most importantly, 23 of the 26 sheriffs in the four selected courts also agreed to be interviewed, although not about specific cases. This gave a total spread across 2 social work regions, 4 sheriff courts, 7 social work districts, about 20 area offices and more than 40 area teams. The research was thus able to identify and examine differences in policy and practice at all levels and stages of the probation process from a variety of perspectives.

1.5 A decline in probation?

We live in an era defined by almost unanimous agreement that prisons are overcrowded, that they don't work, that they are an affront to acceptable standards of humane incarceration, and that every conceivable support should be given to dealing with offenders in other ways. This is attested in, *inter alia*, the earnest discussions about the utility of electronic tagging, through to the Government green paper, *Punishment, Custody and the Community* (HMSO, 1988). At the same time there is loudly voiced official concern about what is seen as the leniency and inappropriateness of many present community schemes for dealing with offenders, most recently illustrated by charges of tax payers' money being wasted on expensive trips and ineffective 'treatment programmes' for young offenders.

What has happened to the senior non-custodial, non-monetary penalty, the probation order, as the debate about law and order and the punishment of offenders has gained momentum and gradually taken centre stage in official government policy? Looking back 40 years, records show that in Scotland, in the 1950s and 1960s, the great majority of probation disposals related to young people under 16. With the introduction of the Childrens' Hearing System in April 1971 there began a dramatic decline in probation disposals for this age group; whereas under 16s accounted for 74% of all such disposals in 1955, they accounted for only 6% in 1972 and only 2% by the beginning of the 1980s. The new legal and administrative framework for helping 'troubled and troublesome' children dealt with 17,950 referrals during the first year of its operation alone.

Nevertheless, even when the analysis of trends in the use of probation in Scotland is restricted to adult disposals, it is evident that probation disposals fell both in absolute and relative terms from the beginning of the 1970s. In 1970 nearly 3,000 adults received probation in the Scottish courts, 1.42% of all those sentenced. By 1985, although the absolute figure had fallen only marginally, more significantly, only 0.97% of those sentenced were made the subject of probation orders.

Any decrease in the use of probation must be a source of interest and concern at a time when alternatives to or diversion from custody are at the forefront of public debate. As far back as 1976, in the Howard League policy document, it was noted that:

> At a time when the urgent need is to develop constructive alternatives to incarceration, for a country with the doubtful distinction of having a greater proportion of its population in prison than any other in Western Europe, the probation system is in danger of withering away or becoming a residual method of dealing with young offenders and persons committing a minor breach of the peace (Howard League, 1976, p. 12).

A further concern about the probation situation in Scotland was expressed in their policy document the following year:

> The supervisor is not now an officer of the court but an officer of the local authority. Perhaps this is where part of the problem lies, since the extent to which courts use probation is an expression of their degree of confidence in the supervising officers...the idea of the probation scheme was clearly to ensure that existing standards of practice were maintained and that the courts retained confidence in the service provided to themselves and to those under supervision (Howard League, 1977, p. 8).

Was the decline in the use of probation due to lack of confidence by the courts? Were existing standards of practice being maintained? What kind of service were courts and probationers getting? Given the almost total lack of any systematic knowledge about process and practice any of these areas, the basic question with which we were faced was, what on earth is happening to

8

probation in Scotland? In the rest of this book we attempt to answer this fundamental question.

2 Sheriffs

We are basically looking for help, because sentencing is a very difficult procedure, and you can feel very lonely.

2.1 Offences and offenders·

2.2.1 Types of offence

Most sheriffs said they used probation for a very wide range of offences and that, although the nature of the offence was important, it was not the sole determining factor in coming to a decision about the appropriateness of probation. One sheriff spoke for all when he said:

> We have to try and balance the offender's interests with the public interest. That is certainly a consideration that I very often have in mind. A kind of balance, I have to strike some kind of balance.

About a third of the sheriffs interviewed did rule out probation for violent assault on the grounds that probation would be quite disproportionate to the seriousness of the crime in these circumstances:

> Some acts of violence might be so bad, that to put the offender on probation is really disproportionate to what he has done. There are three primary objects, as I understand it, in sentencing. These are to deter, to reform and to punish. If somebody is slashed from ear to ear and you put the offender on probation, then you are getting it out of proportion.

Some sheriffs had used probation for violent offences however, and particular attention was drawn to the domestic sphere:

Quite serious offences can happen in the domestic sphere, where something can be done and repented on in a few seconds. There I have noticed that probation can be of great assistance. Particularly where there is support from the probation officer for, say, an attacked wife who has half forgiven her spouse and needs a little assistance with the other half.

2.1.2 Types of offender

Rather than trying to identify types of offences which might merit a probation disposal, most sheriffs found it easier to describe the kind of offender for whom probation supervision might be appropriate. A few highlighted the importance of the 'offender career' feeling that probation could be very useful either in the very early stages of offending or much later on for adult recidivists where everything else had failed:

> Sometimes I have people who have been given custodial disposals for a long time, and they come to you on a matter that is not all that serious, and you want to try and break the chain, break the cycle of imprisonment. Now sometimes you give probation in that case.

In general however, it was the type of person the offender was, rather than the stage of the offending career, which was the main focus for consideration. The following illustrations were typical of the kind of person deemed suitable by sheriffs for probation:

> somebody who is easily influenced, easily led, almost approaching feeble minded, who needs encouragement to give up drinking,...to stay away from certain places and certain friends....Probation is particularly suitable for the weak whatever their weakness.

> a person who is in need of a wee bit of support, encouragement, cajoling; requiring the intervention of another person, possibly someone from outside such as a social worker.

> an offender who is prepared to make the effort. The other test I would apply is whether the offender is in some sense an addict, who needs support from someone who will be able to advise and offer counselling - someone who has difficulties in coping.

A number of sheriffs volunteered that women were particularly suitable for probation. A number of reasons were put forward for this. It might be because:

> they are under the influence either of somebody they are living with, or someone who has left them with all sorts of problems...their offending is related more to their general background of problems than anything else.

Or it might just be that it is difficult to think of an alternative when the effect of a custodial sentence is seen as being more severe than with a man (although one sheriff at least had changed his attitude towards this):

> if you take a married woman...and they have a family to bring up and some crime is committed. The consequences of sending the mother to prison are going to be much worse than sending the father to prison. So one of the compromises is to make a probation order. I see it as totally dodging the issue, but it is an understandable way of doing it. I dare say I've done it myself, but I wouldn't now.

2.1.3 Types of social worker

Sheriffs also indicated that the decision to give probation was also related to the kind of supervision they thought offenders were likely to receive. In relation to this there was general agreement that social workers were stronger on the support, counselling and encouragement aspects than on the control and discipline elements of supervision:

> I would allow probation for a deliberately conscious criminal if I thought the social worker might show the person the error of their ways. But I am not aware that there are many social workers of that calibre.

Several sheriffs remembered the days when there were probation officers as opposed to generic social workers:

> the probation officer saw himself as an officer of the court, and he was to some extent a discipliner as well as an adviser. I doubt if I could expect that from the social worker, so I tend to use probation where there is a clear situation on the kind of help and advice and treatment that has to be afforded.

2.2 Social enquiry reports

2.2.1 Special requests

Sheriffs were asked to give their views on the purpose and function of social work reports, what they found most useful in terms of content, and their attitude towards recommendations from the social worker. Just over half stressed the importance of keeping an open mind at this stage and expressed the fear that, in directing social workers to a particular area. other significant aspects of the case might be overlooked. There was also concern that being

13

too specific might be seen as prejudging the case, 'having a wee something in mind when you shouldn't have'. One sheriff spelled out his approach in full:

> when somebody comes before me I would like to know their whole background. I would like to know if they are a deliberate vicious criminal. I would like to make up my mind if they are a weak member of the community. I would like to make up my mind about these matters from two points of view. One to assess the gravity of their offence and, secondly and quite separately, to decide what is the best disposal. And at that stage I have no fixed views...I am looking for information on which I can form views, information which I hope to get from the social worker.

Just under half the sheriffs acknowledged that they did sometimes ask for particular areas to be explored. This might relate to the need for clarification of background circumstances:

> If, for instance, I was told that this person looked after his old granny and loads of relatives down the stairs...I might want that checked.

Or alternatively, information might be required about the nature and availability of treatment and resources which could affect the suitability of probation for a particular offender:

> The only occasion I ever do it is if I am considering probation...I don't put someone on probation unless the social work department has had the opportunity of indicating whether they agree or disagree with that proposition...My feeling is that the social work department has to administer probation and I think it is unfair to foist on them my views if they are not keen on it. Furthermore my somewhat cynical nature suggests that (if that is the case) they are not going to be very enthusiastic about putting it into effect.

2.2.2 Expectations

Nearly all sheriffs had clear views on what they expected from reports and identified a number of areas which they regarded as useful in the difficult task of sentencing. As on remarked 'sentencing is one of the most difficult, impossible functions we perform and we need every assistance'. To this end sheriffs found reports most useful when they 'illuminated the person'. One defined this in full:

> I expect to be able to read in the report about the offender and his family. His history; some detail about educational background, work history, what he does if he is employed. If he is unemployed - and most of them are unemployed of course - how he spends his time, his associates; the

kind of support he gets from his family, and how he is reacting to the offence. I don't want a lot of detail as to the circumstances of the offence, because I should know what the circumstances are.

Some information about the offender's attitude to the offence and the degree of motivation, should probation be given, was also regarded as important, although, in the words of one sheriff, 'it's sometimes difficult to find that in the reports we tend to get'. Sheriffs also wanted a clear picture of what social work resources were available and suggestions about what could be done to help the offender on probation; 'we are basically looking for help, because sentencing is a very difficult procedure, and you can feel very lonely in dealing with sentencing, particularly in difficult cases'.

A key concern was the relevance of information in reports. Although a very small minority of sheriffs thought as much information as possible should be included, for the sheriff to decide what was relevant, most saw this 'sifting' as part of the report writer's role, not least because of the limited time sheriffs have to read reports. This was particularly so in the case of early childhood:

> History of childhood I find of no interest whatsoever...it is not something I would ever take into account in disposing of somebody. And accordingly childhood illnesses, childhood accidents, and to a large extent childhood schooling, is of no interest to me - unless there is something particularly unusual about it. Therefore I find it tiresome to have all that information.

Comments were also made about the style in which some reports were written and the language used. 'Sometimes they are in a language that we find strange, because it is just part of their training to do that; talking about 'siblings' and things like that, a very 'jargonese' sort of thing, which is very off putting

A more substantial problem noted by a number of sheriffs was that reports often tended to be 'pleas in mitigation' although this was not a function of the social enquiry report:

> These are views reflected by many of my colleagues. They may or may not tell you, but they are views they express themselves. I find ridiculous excuses put forward for criminals in social enquiry reports, to the effect, in general, that the crime is not their fault. It is the fault of others. It is the fault of housing; it is the fault of unemployment; it is the fault of the co-accused; it is the fault of the parents; but it is not their fault. Such reports are unrealistic.

This lack of realism is seen as arising partly from a very partial view of the situation:

(the report writer) hasn't heard what the prosecutor has to say, he hasn't seen the detailed charge, he hasn't heard what the defence agent may have said, which may contradict what is stated in the report. The primary thing is the crime itself. What have they done and - thereafter - what is the appropriate penalty?

and partly from an overly 'client oriented' approach:

When the social enquiry report is bad, generally it is because it is out of character with the known facts. And very often, in the face of a record of repeated offending and different disposals ranging from probation, fines, community service... despite his various, as it were, increases in criminal behaviour which his record indicates, we find a proposal that someone has reformed and promises to be of good behaviour. When the report is given to you, one tends to be confident that it doesn't deal with the man's quite evident difficulties.

In discussing their expectations and the usefulness of social enquiry reports, sheriffs were generally agreed that good report writing was 'an art rather than a science' in which experience as well as training played an important part:

You can instruct a social worker in their training what the report ought to contain, what ingredients it ought to have. I don't think that is a very difficult exercise. The subtlety, the sensitivity, the understanding, is something that varies a lot. Sometimes a new social worker's report is very off key.

and:

The value of a report varies not so much by the type of information it contains, because that tends to be fairly standard, but rather by the maturity, experience and capability of the reporter. Some people are more realistic, more understanding than others. I'm not sure that we would necessarily train people into realism and understanding...it is really to do with the quality of the individual reporter as much as anything.

2.2.3 Recommendations in social enquiry reports

In general there was little opposition to social workers making recommendations about disposal, although there were differences of opinion about the necessity of a recommendation, the way it should be made, what it should cover and the influence it has on the sentencing process.

Five sheriffs said they always looked for recommendations from social workers, were strongly influenced by them and tried to follow them whenever possible. A further seven welcomed them provided they were realistic and social workers were clear what they should recommend. One problem however, identified by both groups, was the frequency of unrealistic recommendations for deferred sentence which, it was thought, social workers opted for when they were not sure what to recommend, or when a recommendation of custody contradicted their professional ideology:

> Seven times out of ten I would follow the recommendation unless it is, in my view, ridiculous...the most frequent one is a deferred sentence for a very serious offence which would normally attract a period of imprisonment. I can understand the rationale behind that recommendation on the basis that the social worker doesn't want to be seen by the customer or client as recommending that he go to prison for a long time.

> Quite a large number of social work reports recommend deferred sentence. You know 'deferred sentence for good behaviour'. It seems to me almost like a get out at the end of the day, when you can't think of anything else more appropriate to say. You get to the end of the report and it is just added on almost as an afterthought, you know, see how he behaves in the meantime. It is almost as if there is nothing else they can think of. It's so common you tend to ignore it when you see it, saying 'here it comes again! here's this recommendation again!'

Several sheriffs said, although they understood why social workers sometimes took that view, they regretted any formal policy that social workers should not recommend custody:

> I have been in one area where social workers have taken a policy decision that they never consider or suggest anyone going to prison. I find that very unhelpful because they are precluding one of the things I have to consider.

Three sheriffs only looked for a recommendation when probation might be a suitable option. As one explained:

> I like to know the reaction of the social worker to probation, because I think, ideally, one should have guidance. After all it is the social work department which is going to have to supervise the order.

One sheriff, feeling that social workers were 'mainly concerned with seeing (the offence) through the eyes of the offender' favoured the idea of a negative rather than a positive recommendation:

> for example, if he says that such a course would not be advisable. I would not expect them to go further than that, because the social worker will not have all the facts of the case which I have in court. I am required to take all the facts into account, but he doesn't have to do that. He is not

concerned with the prevalence of the crime, the effect on the victim and so on and so forth.

Finally concern was expressed that social workers can get too anxious about the whole question of recommendations and that the quality of a report did not depend on whether or not a recommendation was made:

> Quite often a report can be very good, not so much in terms of recommendations, I think too much emphasis is placed on that. A report that ends up saying 'I have no recommendation to make in the circumstances' can still be very good. The primary function is the provision of a perceptive, sensitive background. That is really what I would like to see.

> If I am speaking to social workers I would always make the point that they shouldn't regard the recommendation as the main purpose of the report at all. It is, after all, not their function. But if, consistent with the report, there is some relevant suggestion at the end, exception is not taken to that.

2.2.4 Influence of recommendations

Although most sheriffs said their willingness to give probation disposals largely depended on positive recommendations from social workers, most agreed that in practice they had given probation in the absence of a probation recommendation or where an alternative disposal had been suggested. The following incidence was cited as one example:

> I had this case of a 21 year old woman. She was on some charges of theft and she was looking after her two children by two different fathers, neither of whom she was associating with. The final paragraph of the social enquiry report was 'this person does not require social work supervision'. I thought 'I can hardly think of a better person to have social work supervision'. That is the sort of absurdity one gets.

He continued:

> In an ideal world one should only give probation when it is recommended, but there seem to me to be cases which cry out for it...they are so reluctant to recommend. You see the recommendation in that case was 'deferred sentence' without any sort of supervision, which seemed to me to be a pretty poor sort of recommendation on the whole.

A curious 'reluctance to recommend' was noted by a number of sheriffs, with a minority voicing a suspicion that this was geared more towards social work resources than the needs of the offender. Several others felt that, even when it appeared to be a suitable option, there was little point in making an order if the social worker had indicated that there was little to be gained from it:

> Sometimes I get the impression that there should be probation and yet the report indicates otherwise. I sometimes wonder if the reason is lack of resources or some other cause. Quite often the recommendation is deferred sentence and that's really just leaving the accused to be of good behaviour hopefully, and if he is, nothing much will happen to him...and quite often, from the report, you get the impression more could be done.

Sheriffs, in the small courts particularly, acknowledged that knowing the social worker who had written the report could be influential:

> We have an excellent service and reports here...and if they recommend probation I invariably give it. I trust the social workers in this area because, even in a year or so, I have got to know them and the style of reports they produce. They are right down to earth and don't try to make light of things. So if there is a recommendation I try to follow it.

Even where the recommendation is a 'bit odd', knowing the writer can make a difference:

> In a place of that size you know the social workers. And if...(one of them) makes a recommendation which perhaps on the face of it looks a bit odd, I know the chap. I know he is sensible; I know he is experienced; and I know that he knows me and would think twice about it.

It is of course difficult to know whether these more 'influential recommendations' stemmed from more direct dialogue and realistic mutual understanding between the sheriffs and social workers serving the small courts, or whether social workers were simply tailoring the content and style of reports and recommendations to suit the known idiosyncrasies of particular sheriffs.

2.3 Expectations of social work service

2.3.1 Frequency of supervision

Nearly all the sheriffs interviewed thought that probationers should be seen by the social worker within two weeks of the disposal. Immediacy was thought to be important both to demonstrate the interest of the court and the social work department, and to set the tone for future contact anything beyond that would give the clear impression that the court - or the social worker - wasn't really too interested. I should have thought that future contact with the probationer would be difficult if there was a great delay between the order and the matter being taken up direct. I would have thought it was an absolute priority that the probationer be seen within two weeks.

Another reason was to maximize the motivation of the offender, to 'strike while the iron is hot':

it is then they are at the height of their sensitivity having just been in court and having, as they see it, just missed a custodial sentence. It won't take very long for that feeling to wear off, and I think it is important to get them right away.

However the actual experience of sheriffs, particularly in the larger courts, did not live up to their expectations. One mentioned cases where 'there has been no contact for months, and that's clearly a weakness in the system'. Another knew a probationer for whom 'eleven weeks had gone by and he hadn't seen hide nor hair of a social worker', and a third told us: 'I had a chap who was placed on probation in January and he wasn't allocated a supervisor till June'.

Although sheriffs were less agreed how often a probationer should be seen after the first interview, there were several points on which there was a general consensus of opinion. Most thought, for example, that contact should be fairly intensive initially, reducing towards the end of the probation period:

I would hope that if the person was responding favourably to the probation situation, it should be possible to ease off the leash gradually, because after all what we are trying to do is to get them to stand on their own feet in a mature way.

Regularity of contact was also regarded as important because 'the person has got to remember he is on probation, and it has to be a constant reminder to him'. It was generally felt however, that actual frequency of contact would necessarily vary according to the type of case and this was a matter best left to the professional judgement of the social worker.

(The social worker) should be experienced enough to know fairly early on how often he is going to require to see the offender, and I leave it entirely to them...as far as I am concerned the administration of a probation order is a matter entirely for the social work department and I don't think it is my function to involve myself in it.

Given the 'tailing off' mentioned by sheriffs, their general expectations of frequency of contact seemed to be very broadly in line with the following guidelines piloted in one region during the period of the research. However, thirteen of the nineteen sheriffs who voiced an opinion on the matter, thought that contact during the first three months should be more frequent than suggested:

> A minimum of five contacts should be made during the first three months, the first of which should take place within one week of receipt of the order, and at least two of which should take the form of a home visit. Thereafter, after review, the level of contact may be adjusted to the needs of each case, but should not be less than monthly.

2.3.2 Social work service to probationers

The prevention of further offences by the probationer was clearly seen by sheriffs as the primary purpose of probation. Having said that, most sheriffs also felt that probation should offer something positive to the probationer. This was usually couched in general terms like 'giving him a positive outlook', 'helping him to become a more worthwhile citizen', 'giving him the opportunity to prove himself', or 'having someone who can help him work out his problems'. Given these general aims, the role of the social worker and the content of supervision was seen very much in terms of a traditional case-work model, based mainly on one-to-one contact, and involving home visits as well as the offender 'reporting' to the office. Only two sheriffs mentioned group work and one of these had considerable reservations:

> I discovered a fellow I had put on probation had been dealt with in a group of probationers. I was appalled and put a stop to it as quickly as possible. I had no idea that that was being done. It certainly wasn't what I intended.

When questioned about the content of supervision, sheriffs' answers fell into several categories which were concerned with both the care and control aspects of the work. Monitoring was regarded as particularly important and was seen as more than just a mechanical checking up:

> the type of supervision that probation should be is...a general supervision rather than one particular aspect of a person's life. I mean, is the court saying that provided you are at the police station at 3 o'clock on a Saturday afternoon, we don't care what you do the rest of your life? That seems to me to be against the whole principle of probation.

The importance of specific practical advice was also mentioned by most sheriffs:

> the most important thing is actually telling the man how to apply for a job, telling him where to go and look for one, or how to get his benefit or

21

whatever. It is much more important than airy-fairy pretending to be a psychiatrist, which is what can often happen.

And hand in hand with this, a more general advice and guidance, with the social worker taking a genuine interest in the everyday life of the offender:

> how they should be conducting themselves in a socially acceptable way. I don't necessarily mean anything to do with morals. By socially acceptable I mean crime free. If a problem arises which could tip the balance and cause the person to commit a crime, I hope (the social worker) could be a mixture of a supervisor and a sort of well intentioned older relative, who is there to keep an eye on things and be strict if strictness is required, but not be a disciplinarian.

For many offenders placed on probation because they have a specific problem, support, encouragement and counselling were seen as important aspects of supervision:

> If they have a specific problem and seek appropriate help, they can often lead a normal life thereafter. It is not always a hopeless situation...they may be severely lacking in their own estimation of self worth and need a lot of propping and supporting, someone to take the strain off their lives.

While most sheriffs were able to discuss their general expectations of supervision, it was evident that they had little idea whether their expectations were being met. Well over half admitted that they had no idea what happened once an order had been made. One sheriff told us:

> I really don't know the first thing about the workings of probation at all, or of what they do. So I can't really say whether they are making proper use of the disposal.

And another remarked:

> I really have a great ignorance of the workings of the thing. I have never met a probation officer, or discussed their approach to the job at all.

Yet another admitted:

> I don't know what service they get...what do they have to do? Do they have to come down at 10 o'clock or what? Or do they have to meet at another place or...well, what kind of things do they discuss?

A small minority of sheriffs were not concerned about their lack of knowledge, feeling that once the disposal had been made 'the ball was in someone else's court'.

> I take the view that if I am told to do this, if it is appropriate to do this, and if there is an Act of Parliament telling me to do it, then I should do it.

If someone else doesn't keep their end up that is really their business and there's nothing I can do about it.

In general however, most sheriffs were keen to have more information, unfavourably comparing the feedback on probation with that on community service:

We don't know what exactly happens. I expect some of us don't use probation as much as we might, because we don't know too much. We know a wee bit about community service, because the principal officer established a super relationship with the sheriffs telling us what was involved and being quite frank about the difficulties.

Sheriffs views about probation supervision in Scotland generally, did not always coincide with their views about the service in their particular court area. In the three smaller courts, all but one of the sheriffs were reasonably well satisfied and some were extremely positive in their comments; none was dissatisfied. In contrast, in the large court, only three out of seventeen sheriffs said they were even reasonably satisfied, and over a third expressed unqualified dissatisfaction. It must be noted however, that nearly half of the large court sheriffs acknowledged that their rating of the service was extremely subjective. Dissatisfaction was based on personal experience rather than on any real knowledge of the actuality of probation practice, and where satisfaction was expressed it was usually on the assumption that all was going well in the absence of any negative feedback.

2.3.3 Links with social work departments

Sheriffs lack of knowledge about probation supervision raises the question of the links between courts and social work departments. In three of the four courts formal links were usually through the court social workers, and the importance of their role was emphasised by sheriffs, particularly in the large court where the opportunity for individual links was difficult. The other court was serviced by a social work team, with social workers attending court on a rota basis. This was efficient in obtaining reports on time, but something of the personal touch was lost:

there is a remoteness about it...I liked the times when one could ask questions arising from the report, what something meant, or something one thought of that they hadn't mentioned, and what did they think of that, and so on. I found that very useful...I miss that.

In the large court most sheriffs made mention of the liaison committee and thought it worked reasonably well (although few seemed to know much about it). One or two said they knew virtually nothing about the committee and

23

several others felt there was still room for considerable improvement in communication. Most frequently mentioned was the need for more feedback about whether matters registered at the committee had been considered or acted upon in any way.

As well as formal links with the social work department, the desirability of links with individual social workers was discussed with sheriffs. Interestingly, there was a marked contrast between the views of sheriffs in the smaller courts and those in the large court. In the smaller courts such links were generally seen as contributing to a mutually responsive service, and were both possible and used in practice:

> If I get a report where either I'm going to do something the social worker won't approve of, or where I've thought of something he hasn't covered I just phone and say 'well, I'm thinking of this', or 'I've looked at the report and can you tell me this', or 'what do you think of that'. But, there again, you can only do that in a small court.

In the large court links with individual workers were seen as practically impossible, because of the large area covered and the enormous number of social workers involved. Nor were such links generally regarded as desirable:

> I would be rather loath to be involved in a two way dialogue with the social worker...because I feel that what is being said may well be of importance and...I think it would be wrong if it was thought that the court was in cahoots with the social worker.

2.4 Progress and completion of probation orders

2.4.1 Use of breach

All twenty three sheriffs commented on social workers' knowledge and use of breaching provisions in respect of both commission of a further offence and non-compliance. In terms of satisfaction, nine indicated that, as they usually only saw those who had been breached (and none of those who perhaps should have been), they had only part of the total picture and could not make a judgement. Ten sheriffs were at least reasonably satisfied and four were generally dissatisfied.

Several points were repeatedly raised about social workers' handling of breach procedures. First, it was recognised that social workers had to use their own discretion in deciding whether the terms of an order had been breached, particularly in relation to non-compliance:

obviously there are going to be failures along the line. People are not going to respond the first time and they are going to have to be cajoled. I don't think that is a reason for breaching, the fact that the response is not as high as you'd like it to be. I think the social worker has to be the final judge.

Second, sheriffs expected social workers to report breaches, even though they might simultaneously recommend continuing the order:

I would prefer a social worker to report a breach on an order I have made, even if the recommendation was to continue. Because, very often, I warn them...the next time it may not be a question of continuing the order. I much prefer a social worker to (do this) than sweep it under the carpet.

It was important too, for breaches to be reported promptly:

I have noticed some very late breaches. Nine months or something have expired, before whatever has gone wrong is finding its way back to me. I would hope that could be speeded up because I think the court should be seen as playing a constructive part in dealing with the offender who is to be rehabilitated in the process.

This sheriff commented further on the need for the court to be taken into the consultation process, reflecting the general view that the court should be used constructively, even if it was only, to quote another sheriff, 'to enable social workers use the court as the big, bad wolf if necessary'.

I always tell them that they will be breached if they don't do as they are told. So I think it is important that, if they don't do what they are told, then they will be breached. I certainly put people on probation on the theory they will be brought back if they breach it, if they don't co-operate.

2.4.2 Early discharge

While one sheriff had no particular view, twenty two said they would always consider requests for early termination orders. Some however, were more enthusiastic than others. Only three sheriffs, all in the large court, said they almost always granted requests of this kind. In respect of a one year order for example:

My understanding is that social workers would expect that, after nine months supervising properly, they would have got to where they wanted. If someone came back and said something like 'so and so has got a job, settled down, got a house', I would think it would be very sensible to say 'that's fine, give them the credit'. They like to think of it as having three

25

months off their sentence. I would always think the spirit of probation was that the length of the order was the maximum.

Another added:

I always grant it...on the basis that the social worker knows the position, knows what's going on, and other than the 'clearing the bottom drawer of the filing cabinet syndrome', which I think is easily detectable, I am more than happy to discharge an order if it has worked. In fact I am really quite pleased on the basis that it was the right disposal.

Six sheriffs, across the four courts, were not keen on terminating orders early, reasoning that if they had given what they considered an appropriate length of order in the first place, it was important for the probationer to maintain progress over that period of time. Again speaking of a one year order, one sheriff commented:

You see, one of the things about probation, and I say this to a punter when I put him on probation, is that it really means probation. "You have to prove yourself, and that means you have to stay out of trouble while you are on probation, and that means for a year".

The majority view was neither for or against, with sheriffs indicating that they kept an open mind on the matter and judged each case entirely on its merits. As one sheriff explained:

I decide from the report whether it should be terminated... sometimes I grant the recommendation and sometimes I don't. If I want further information I ask for it. It depends how the probationer is doing and why they want to terminate the probation. Again, I would look at the papers and remind myself of the circumstances and decide whether or not the care and control has expired or whatever, according to the individual case.

2.4.3 Completion reports

Thirteen of the fifteen sheriffs who commented welcomed the idea of a completion report from the social worker at the end of the probation period and identified a number of possible benefits. These included learning more about the content and practice of probation, raising the quality of supervision, and increasing the confidence of the court in making probation disposals in the future.

Sheriffs were almost equally divided about the desirability and feasibility of progress reports during the order. Those against the idea thought that social workers should be left to supervise without the interference of the court, arguing that the sanction of breaching was always there if things went wrong. Even those in favour acknowledged the immense practical problems due to the sheer volume of work which would be necessary, both for the courts and the social work departments.

2.4.4 Defining a successful outcome

It might seem a fairly simple matter to define a successful probation order, but sheriffs weren't so sure. Perhaps somewhat surprisingly, only two took the strictly legalistic view that a probation order could only be regarded as a success if no further offending had occurred during the period of the order. A few more regarded the absence of further offences as the major, but not sole criterion:

> A successful order is not just an order that has been completed without being breached. That's the criminal level, isn't it? A successful order would be one where the probationer benefited, firstly to the extent where they wouldn't reoffend and secondly, to become a better person - to encourage him in that. Thirdly, if he took something out of it, I would say that is successful.

Slightly more sheriffs went further, holding the view that the main criterion for success was the degree of improvement and change shown by the probationer:

> I would consider probation to be successful if, at the end of the period, the social worker was able to say, 'this guy is more responsible now. This guy or girl has offended a couple of times, but the frequency of offending is dropping, they have got a job, or their lifestyle has changed, or their peer group has changed, or they are out of the drug scene or whatever'. That, to me. is a successful probation order. The fact that a person reoffends does not make it an unsuccessful probation order.

2.5 The individuality of sheriffs

The closer links with social workers, and higher level of service in the smaller courts, appeared to result in increased knowledge and satisfaction about probation on the part of sheriffs. How far this was reflected in sentencing policy and a greater use of probation, the small scale, inductive nature of the research did not allow us to say. It was interesting however, that in the court where social workers had the closest individual links with sheriffs, provided a high level of service to probationers, and deployed mainly 'authority based' models of practice (see chapter 5), sheriffs were more satisfied with the social work service than those in any other court. It is possible that this could

account for the number of very high tariff offenders given probation in this area. Indeed, it seemed from interviews with both social workers and sheriffs there, that the latter were more likely to make a probation disposal in a high risk case if the recommendation came from a social worker who was known and trusted, and who had argued a good case.

Perhaps the most striking feature to emerge from the sheriff interviews however, was the individuality of sheriffs themselves. We were unable to identify clearly delineated 'types' of sheriff in the way that we were able, for example, to classify probationers and social work service. On any one issue, there were always some sheriffs in support, a few neutral, and others adamantly in opposition; furthermore there was no real personal consistency. There was no obvious ideological division either, between sheriffs in large and small courts, urban and rural areas, or between 'old' sheriffs, who had worked with a separate probation service, and newer ones, who hadn't.

In short, the picture was both confused and confusing. Sheriffs collectively - and occasionally individually - could appear contrary; on the one hand supporting more recommendations for probation; on the other regarding other elements of the report as much more crucial, occasionally to the extent of definitely not wanting a recommendation. Sometimes stressing the importance of knowing much more about supervision; at others feeling it was not their business, and much better left entirely to the social worker.

Finally however, although the fact that no clear pattern emerges may be a source of analytic irritation to the researcher, it does serve to demonstrate the continuing independence of the judiciary, and perhaps the independence of justice itself.

3 Probationers

Thinking back now I think probation has saved my life. Technically speaking, it's saved my life.

3.1 Introduction

The 86 probationers in the study were followed up using a variety of methods. Social workers were asked about the background and history of each probationer, the factors which had led to their offending, and their response to probation supervision. Case records, social enquiry reports and other secondary sources were also examined and analysed. From the social work perspective therefore we were able to follow the progress of all 86 cases.

Examining the probation process from the offender's perspective proved somewhat more difficult. Although we had initially planned to interview every probationer several times during the course of the order, in practice, despite persistent attempts, we only managed to do this with 43 probationers. About half of those we failed to interview either refused, or were breached and in custody before contact could be made. Well over a third had either disappeared, moved away or repeatedly failed to turn up for interview, and the remaining few cases were closed before we could see them. One probationer died early in the order.

The 50% response rate obviously raises the question of how representative of the total sample our interviews with probationers were. Although the interviewees did not vary significantly from the total sample on the main selection criteria of age, gender, offence type and court area, there was some difference in the proportion of probationers from each of the four offender categories we drew up. We were able to interview about three quarters of all first and early offenders, but only about half of the adult recidivists, and only one third of young persistent offenders.

It is likely too, given the reasons why some interviews were not carried out, that those probationers who were seen had particular characteristics; more committed, more co-operative, less mobile and having a better relationship with their supervisors than other probationers. The results of the interviews therefore, taken on their own, may well give too positive a picture of the probation process. Their value lies mainly in providing a supplement and a check on the information obtained from other sources, and in giving a deeper insight into what probation means to those at the receiving end.

3.2 Probationers' attitudes

3.2.1 To the problems which led to their offending

A third of the probationers saw their offence as arising from acute social, financial or personal problems:

> I had got into a lot of debt and people kept hassling. And there was one, I kept telling him I was going to pay it so much as I could afford. And they didn't agree to this, and kept phoning and everything. And these people I was working for had found a cheque and I had forged their name on it to pay off the people that was hassling me for the debt.

About the same number saw the cause of the problem as alcohol or, less commonly, drug abuse - sometimes a combination. In most cases this was a long standing problem, sometimes accompanied by personal or psychiatric problems:

> I had a problem with drink...drinking, and I wasn't capable of looking after my child. they put me on probation and to attend these AA meetings.

A few probationers attributed their offending to keeping 'bad company', sometimes intentionally, at other times unwittingly:

> It started off with a giro, right? Now there was a guy came running out of a pub, we know him, right? 'Do you want to run in with that? I'm waiting for my sister.' I says 'Aye, I will'...and I went in and cashed it and the next thing I know is there's court cases about this giro. The giro had been stolen.

A few did not acknowledge any problem, or were uncertain what it was:

> [Q. Are you finding it helpful? Are you finding you are able to sort out your problems?] Yes. [Q. Can you tell me a bit more about that?] Well

I've come to terms with the problem. [Q. What do you think the problem is basically?] Well, at the moment I don't really know.

3.2.2 To the court and their probation order

Probationers' feelings about their court appearance varied from humiliation and fear, through anxiety, to comparative confidence (from experienced offenders who knew the system and felt they had a good case). Needless to say, the reaction to getting probation showed a corresponding variation.

A quarter felt unmixed relief at what they saw as a positive outcome and the chance for help it afforded:

> It was a great relief because at the time when this all happened I didn't know where to turn. I was so sort of, not mentally disturbed, but I mean disturbed sort of thing...trapped. I had never come across this sort of thing before.

About half felt relief at avoiding custody, seeing probation as a comparatively easy option. As one put it:

> Well I didn't really want to get probation, but I thought it was better than getting a prison sentence.

Another agreed:

> It is easy. I mean, it's not like community service...that's easy as well, but you've got to go out twice a week and you've got to work 12 hours. A fine you need to pay out of your own money, but probation doesn't cost you anything, you know what I mean? It's not as if you spend a lot of time with it.

A few probationers had very mixed feelings. Whilst relieved they had avoided custody, they nevertheless did not welcome probation, either because of previous experience or because it had been presented to them in a very negative light:

> I really felt terrible...'cause I thought they were really taking my bairns off me. I thought they were going to be there every third day. I really thought they were going to come down on me quite heavy.

Two probationers felt disappointed because they had expected a different non-custodial disposal:

> I wanted community service. There were no places so I got probation instead...I used to work with children. That was it, I wanted to work.

One or two experienced probationers appeared to have been fairly confident of the outcome and to have used the system to their advantage:

> The social worker was recommending a deferred sentence...I says I would rather get probation...I thought there's not much chance of me getting a deferred sentence, whereas with probation at least, if there's a chance of that, then I'm not going to prison. So I thought I would be better going for in between. [Q. Did the social worker agree with that?]...Yes, but not for them reasons. He says I wanted it to give me a bit of support, but when you get down to brass tacks it was better than going to jail. I thought it was just common sense.

3.2.3 To the requirements of the order

Although all the social workers interviewed said they explained the requirements of a probation order at the first interview with the probationer, probationers' knowledge of the requirements was very variable. The majority referred only to having to stay out of trouble and see their social worker regularly. Some added that they had to discuss any problems with the social worker. A typical response was:

> I was expecting rules and conditions and all that, but there were really only two; don't get into any trouble and attend regularly.

Only a handful mentioned having to inform a change of address or employment, and most of these knew they could be taken back to court if they failed to comply. In all about a quarter had detailed knowledge of breach procedures and penalties, and most of these were experienced offenders.

Apart from their knowledge of the requirements of the order, probationers varied greatly in their commitment to them. We judged probationers' commitment, not only by their direct responses, but on independent ratings by two researchers, based on their overall impression of each interview. About half were rated as having a high degree of commitment - making the most of the chance for help, keeping to the requirements of the order, co-operating fully and working actively on problems.

A few were rated as having a superficial degree of commitment - keeping to the 'letter of the law' by conscientious fulfilment of the requirements but with little understanding or intention to change. Slightly more had a low degree of commitment with no intention at all of changing their way of life. Probation, for this group, represented an easy option and adherence to requirements was minimal.

3.3 Probationers' views

3.3.1 On their contact with the social worker

Almost every probationer reported an arrangement of seeing the social worker weekly or fortnightly initially, reducing to every four or six weeks as the order progressed. In fact most probationers seemed satisfied with the level of contact in that there were only three complaints on this score; one of difficulty in contacting the social worker because of an obstructive receptionist, a second of a social worker repeatedly missing appointments, and a third of a social worker deliberately avoiding contact.

Almost all probationers saw their social worker regularly by appointment, with a few doing so on a more casual drop-in basis. In these cases frequency varied from almost daily to once every few months so supervision might be very intensive at one end of the scale to highly inadequate on the other. Some probationers, for example, were merely left to contact the social worker when desired:

> Because I was working he didn't really bother much. He doesn't see me that often...at first it was generally about once a month, but after that it drifted away. It was only on a need to see basis. If I needed to see him I could phone.

A more systematic drop-in system operated in one office, where it was clear that regular attendance was expected:

> I've not really got a set thing. It's maybe every week or every two weeks...it's better that way than to be here every week or else...I have to come but it doesn't bother me 'cause it's doing me good.

There were no firm shared rules about the place of contact. About a third of the probationers were seen both at home and in the social work office - sometimes for 'casework' reasons, sometimes for convenience. A quarter were seen only at home, because of various family commitments and a third were seen only at the office. In a small number of cases other locations were used, such as local cafes or, in one instance, the social worker's car. Most probationers expressed satisfaction about the meeting arrangements and some were appreciative of the social worker's efforts to meet their particular needs.

3.3.2 On the helpfulness of the social worker

The majority of probationers found probation more helpful than expected for a variety of reasons. For some it was because the social worker was more flexible and friendly than expected:

33

I am surprised how easy it is to talk to him and get on. I would have thought it would have been a lot more official if that is the word...It makes a lot of difference. You feel he is on your side rather than just there to check up.

Others received more help than anticipated:

I thought that probation was just that somebody told you what to do. I didn't think it was talking over your problems, talking about things. I think that helps a lot.

Some found supervision more challenging than expected, discovering that the social worker couldn't be conned, but confronted the probationer over problems, demanded commitment and pushed for change.

I had a drink problem but I've stopped it...she brought me round to it. She explained it all, pointed out all the charges that have been involved with drink, just about every one...See, I really couldn't see that myself.

Just under a quarter found supervision much as expected - all had previous experience of probation in the course of a long history of offending behaviour. Finally, a small minority were disappointed with the supervision they received; two had expected more interventionist help, one felt the social worker was hostile and unfair, and one thought probation was too easy.

All probationers were asked what kind of help they had received from their social worker. Although different kinds of supervision were described, a number of key elements which probationers found helpful were commonly mentioned and are outlined below in order of the frequency with which they were mentioned.

Nearly all probationers mentioned the importance of the social worker as somebody they could turn to; talk to, confide in, discuss things with, obtain information from, and let off steam to if necessary. Just having someone there was important to many:

It gives me peace of mind knowing he's there if anything goes wrong...him just being there...I just need to pick up the phone and he will be able to help me out.

Most probationers, too, emphasised the value of practical help with problems of finance, accommodation or job finding. Mention was also frequently made of effective liaison with other agencies on the probationer's behalf:

That's the kind of thing that helps because we are getting nowhere but she knows the ropes...she knows all the ins and outs of it.

And in another instance:

He told me about this job. I had this form and filled it in. He gave me a reference...there's no way I'd have been able to do that. I've been in and out of the job centre for three years and nobody has ever said 'right, we'll try that one'. So that's a gain.

Other elements of supervision identified as useful by probationers were advice - whether direct or indirect - and help in sorting out problems and thinking straight:

I couldn't see a way round it...when you're so upset and things are happening, you don't see the right avenues to take, you know, you are not concentrating right. But when you get things sorted, you can say 'well, I'll do such and such'.

Appreciated too, were social workers who forced probationers to confront problems head on:

She put pressure on me to stop drinking and made me see what it was doing to me...that [it] was just going to ruin my life. She kept drumming that into my head. It was good support - it made me want to change.

Occasionally, respondents received help from the social worker which extended well beyond the call of duty:

She sometimes comes in her own time, taking the kids to the swimming, or taking them out for a wee while for me, you know, whenever she can manage.

A minority of probationers complained about their social workers and amongst these there was considerable agreement about the areas of dissatisfaction. Most frequently mentioned was the kind of supervision which consisted mainly of social chit-chat, with nothing really happening:

Probation isn't doing anything for me at all...I'm just coming to tell her I'm doing nothing...that I'm not getting into trouble. She says 'that's fine, cheerio! Nice to see you again - come back next week'.

Others recalled failure to follow up practical advice when necessary; in short, failure to 'deliver the goods'.

She says, 'write a letter to the Social Security and ask them again'. So I wrote away and got a letter saying no and she says, 'what you should do is appeal against it' and that was that...The very first time I met her she said, 'I'll give you a letter for the Red Cross or something so that you can get stuff for the children'. Still not had any word and I'd never ask her again - I get embarrassed.

Also criticised were attempts by social workers to give specialist advice outwith their competence, such as drug, marital or sex counselling, or intensive 'casework' help in the form of exploration of early childhood experience.

> He keeps bringing it back and says there's a lot more to come...he said one week, 'we'll go right back to when you were a kid with your mother and father'. I asked him what my mother and father had to do with it. I didn't like that because my parents are both dead. They had nothing to do with it. I don't see why they should come into it...my father was a hard working man and he brought us up the best he could with the money he was getting.

Only two probationers had been offered group supervision by their social worker - neither welcomed it:

> I'm not a person who likes groups. I don't really feel I've got to go on being in groups for the rest of my life. I don't want to be a regular attender in group sessions.

3.3.3 On the attitude of social workers

For many probationers their social worker's attitude towards them was as important as the content of the help offered. Again there was considerable agreement about the particular attitudes which were seen as positive and helpful. A good social worker, above all, was seen as friendly and informal; more like a friend than a social worker but, at the same time, having an underlying authority of which the probationer was always aware:

> He has the authority but it doesn't seem like that at all. You get a coffee and a smoke and a relax. It is not apparent...I see friendship which is easier to deal with, rather than laying down rules and me just sitting there.

Other highly valued attributes were the ability to listen, to be sympathetic, accepting and trustworthy.

> There's none finer...she can talk like a normal person to a normal person. I think you could go to her and say, 'look, I'm needing a wee bit help' and she would understand. Even if she didn't understand she'd still sit and listen...I think you expect that of a social worker. They should sit and listen and never be shocked no matter what anybody says.

Social workers who seemed genuinely interested, offering encouragement and support, and taking the probationer's ideas seriously, were also highly valued:

> He has been extremely supportive. He could have said, 'don't give me this' but he didn't, he has been extremely encouraging. I'm saying I believe

Jesus Christ has changed my life. He could have said, 'we have a crank here' but he didn't. He has been extremely supportive, and makes enquiries about how I have progressed along those lines.

Straightforward plain speaking by social workers was also thought to be helpful, particularly if mutually allowed:

If she's got something to say, she'll say it, just straight to the point. If I'm in the wrong, she'll say it...she'll not say, 'that's right'. And I'll say what I think. I mean she's not sort of, 'I'm the boss and you can't answer me back' sort of thing. You can say back what you think yourself.

Social workers who were perceived as firm, not allowing probationers to 'get away with it', inspired respect, as did those who were described as 'pushy', demanding change and effort from the probationer:

She pushed me a lot of the time. I think she knew I needed that push, and that has helped me...you need a bit of somebody pushing you all the time.

The qualities valued by probationers reflected closely the 'care and control' strands of traditional probation practice. In some cases the 'care' aspect appeared to dominate the social worker-probationer relationship and authority was not in evidence. Many probationers however, were well aware of both strands and apparently experienced no conflict between them.

While there was a good deal of consensus as to what attitudes were helpful, there was less agreement about unhelpful attitudes, although individual probationers did complain about social workers (often previous ones) who were judgmental, arrogant and domineering. Interestingly, probationers had little respect for social workers who were 'not strict enough'.

3.3.4 On additional requirements

Seventeen of the probationers interviewed were subject to additional requirements as part of their probation order. Nine of these related to attendance for psychiatric treatment, and five to alcohol or drug counselling. Two had to make compensatory payments and one was required to undertake voluntary work and pay a fine. Only 12 probationers mentioned the additional requirements and only seven said the requirement had been monitored by their social worker.

About half of those subject to additional requirements thought the extra condition linked with social work help had been beneficial. Monitoring of the extra requirement by the social worker was not at all resented by probationers who were committed, and who regarded the social worker as having a genuine interest in their welfare:

It's their job. They've got to check up on me...it's the same as if I started playing up and didn't go to my probation meetings. She'd have to tell the court.

Those probationers who found attendance at a particular centre or clinic unhelpful or unnecessary, generally found their social workers flexible about continuing:

She knew I was doing well and staying off the drink...my life's organised and I can cope with things. but if I take the urge to drink again, I've got to phone her up and she'll put me on to someone.

A few probationers felt the element of compulsion was counter productive:

Just because the court says it, it isn't necessarily a good thing. It might be one of the clauses of your probation and because you don't want to go to jail you do it, but you don't really want to. You should go to the centre because you want to be helped, not because you're forced into it. I went before I was put on probation...but had it been one of the conditions, then I don't think I would have liked it.

Two probationers, both of whom were hostile to their social workers on several grounds, resented 'being checked up on':

What really bugs me is that when he goes to see my doctor, he always sees him before me and never tells me the truth. He shouldn't have the right to do it.

She phones them up to see if I'm attending the meetings. I don't think it's right. I'm going to the meetings, she's no need to phone up to see if I'm there or not. It's nothing to do with her.

Finally, one complained that having to attend two agencies confused things because, in his case, the requirement to attend a psychiatric clinic had been discharged before the probation order was finally allocated to a social worker, six months after the disposal had been made:

I couldn't understand the social worker wanting to see me like that. It [the letter] said about probation, so I couldn't understand it. I thought I was coming off the psychiatrist, I thought my time was up...and then I had to go to my social worker, probation officer.

3.4 Responses to probation

From the probationer interview data it was possible to identify some broad response patterns to probation, from which we constructed six 'typical' vignettes, outlined below. The first four represent mainly positive responses to the service received, while the final two reflect the feelings of those who were less happy with their experience of probation. The vignettes are neither discrete or immutable; some types overlap, some probationers fell into no readily defined pattern, and in two instances probationers changed their response pattern during the course of the order.

3.4.1 A cry for help

Here the offence has arisen as a result of acute social, personal, or financial problems, which the probationer recognises and for which help is welcomed. The probationer is basically law abiding, unconnected with any criminal network, and is frightened and disturbed by the initial involvement with the police and the subsequent court appearance. Being 'put on probation' is a real crisis and the social worker is viewed as someone who can rescue them from this situation. Typically such probationers reported great changes in their lives as a result of the intervention provided by the order and were very satisfied with the service they received.

3.4.2 A breathing space

This is the term used by these probationers to describe their experience of probation. While they share many of the characteristics of the previous group, they differ essentially in that they see themselves as responsible for any change that occurs, rather than viewing the social worker as the solution to their problems. While they are grateful for social work support and interest, it is the 'breathing space' which probation gives them to work actively on their own problems, which is seen as the key to success.

3.4.3 Helpful deterrence

These probationers see themselves as having offended through marginal involvement in criminal activities - getting into bad company or 'taking a chance'. They do not see themselves as criminals and, as they do not regard their problems as major ones, are not desperate for help. Initially they may resent probation as disproportionate to their offence. However, they do have some commitment to avoid offending in future, and therefore see probation as a deterrent and an incentive to keep on the rails. It also offers a framework for help with any practical problems they may have. Probationers who responded in this way reported some change for the better as a result of probation and were generally satisfied with the service received.

3.4.4 Turning point

Some probationers genuinely feel that the order represents a real turning point in their lives. They link a long record of offending to alcohol or drug abuse, or to personal or psychiatric problems. While they welcome probation, at least partly, as an alternative to custody, they also see it as a chance to make a fresh start, and to break from their habitual pattern of offending, and a life in and out of prison.

These offenders recognise that they have serious problems and see social work intervention as a last chance for real help. Their commitment is high, they are very much aware of the probation contract and its sanctions, and co-operate reasonably well. The quality of supervision is particularly important in maintaining their commitment, and these probationers welcome straightness, plain speaking and competence from the social worker, recognising their need for controls and incentives. In general probationers in this group reported considerable change in their lives as a result of probation and were very positive about the supervision they had received.

3.4.5 Irrelevant

These probationers do not really consider they have a problem. The offence is seen either as trivial, as long past, or as part of a history of offending which is simply regarded as a way of life. Probation is welcomed as a means of avoiding custody , but is not really seen as impinging on their lives in any way. Since they do not think they have any need for help and certainly have no intention of changing, it is simply irrelevant.

Not surprisingly, these probationers reported little change as a result of the order, and most were lukewarm or even scornful about the social work service they received. Many had received extensive social work help in the past in the form of Childrens' Hearing supervision, sometimes, in the case of younger probationers, from the same social worker as recommended and was supervising the current probation order. For them, social work supervision, like offending, was simply regarded as part of life.

3.4.6 Intrusive

Like those offenders who see probation as irrelevant, those who see it as intrusive think that probation supervision should not impinge on their lives. They mostly deny any problem, but if they do acknowledge one, think it is better dealt with by another agency. In any event, it is none of the social worker's business. Attempts to involve them in recognising or working on any problems identified by the social worker, are seen as an invasion of privacy. Such probationers, unsurprisingly, reported little change as a result of probation, unless it was for the worse. Indeed, several were quite hostile to their social workers and saw supervision as a punitive process.

3.5 Probationer responses and offender categories

3.5.1 Offender categories

The 86 probationers who formed the basis of the study varied widely in their previous offending history. This was obtained mainly from case records, which were very variable in the information they contained. Sometimes conviction lists were available, but in other cases previous offences had to be gleaned from social enquiry reports, supplemented by information from the probationer or the social worker. In all cases however we were able to get a picture of the probationer's offending background, sometimes stretching back many years.

In terms of offending history, probationers fell easily into four main categories. The first of these we termed First Offenders for the obvious reason that they had no previous convictions, although a few had been through the Childrens' Hearings on grounds of truancy or neglect. Some 26 probationers fell into this category. Nine of the 86 fell into the second category of Early Offenders, who had one or two previous convictions, and a number of whom, like the first group, had appeared before the Childrens' Panel.

A third category of Young Persistent Offenders comprised 25 probationers all under 21. They all had three or more previous convictions and, very frequently, a long history of involvement with the Childrens' Hearings, often on offence grounds. Finally there were the Adult Recidivists, all over 21, with at least three and often over 30 previous convictions.

Of the 26 first offenders, 17 were tried in the small courts, and only 9 in the large court. Of the 9 early offenders, only 4 were tried in the small courts, with the remaining 5 in the large court. Some 11 of both the young persistent offenders and of the adult recidivists were seen in the small courts, with 14 of the former and 15 of the latter seen in the large court.

3.5.2 Probationer response related to offender category

Although we were only able to interview 43 of the 86 probationers in the study, we wanted to see if there was any observable link between probationer response and offender category. Of the 17 first offenders, half (8) exhibited the 'cry for help' response; 1 the need for a 'breathing space', and a further 3 feeling the order would function as 'helpful deterrence'. Only 5 of the 17 had a negative attitude to their probation, with 2 finding the order 'intrusive', and 3 'irrelevant'.

41

The 6 early offenders were also, on balance, positive about their order, with 2 finding it gave them a 'breathing space', and another 2 feeling the order would function as 'helpful deterrence'. The other 2 thought probation 'irrelevant'. The 12 adult offenders were evenly divided between positive and negative attitudes, with 1 finding probation something of a 'breathing space', and 5 that it was a 'turning point' in their life. Of the 6 who were negative about probation, 4 thought it 'irrelevant' and 2 'intrusive'. Finally and perhaps predictably, of the 7 young persistent offenders, on 2 were positive (both seeing the order as a 'turning point'), with the 5 remaining all defining probation as 'irrelevant'.

It is clear that the majority of first and early offenders interviewed, responded positively to probation. In contrast, the majority of young persistent offenders responded much more negatively. It is perhaps interesting that the two in this category who showed a more positive response were the two oldest and, in terms of both age and personal circumstances, had much more in common with probationers in the adult recidivist group.

Responses in the latter category were much more mixed. Yet the overall pattern however does tend to suggest that positive responses to probation are more likely to arise in probationers who have particular kinds of offending histories. This suggestion must of course be treated with extreme caution, based as it is on a small and skewed sample. Nevertheless the results are of interest in several respects.

First, they support the views expressed by sheriffs, social workers and probationers themselves, most of whom suggested that probation was particularly suitable for early offenders. Sheriffs and social workers also felt that some long-standing offenders, who had reached a stage in their lives when they genuinely wanted to 'break the habit', were good candidates for probation. Finally many social workers expressed the view that the one type of offender for whom probation was not suitable, was the young persistent offender who had already been the object of extensive social work intervention.

The results are also of interest as much for the exceptions as the rules. In cases where probationers responded differently to supervision than might have been expected from their offending history, there appeared to be at least a partial explanation for this in terms of the kind of supervision they received. Probationers themselves, when asked what they thought made for a successful probation order, identified two factors; a well motivated probationer and a good social worker. We shall examine the interaction between these two factors later in the book. First however, let us take a closer look at those who carry out the supervision of probationers.

4 Supervising officers

4.1 Introduction: probation in a generic social work department

The 86 probation cases which we looked at in the previous chapter were held by a total of 57 social workers. As outlined in the introduction, all were interviewed at least once and often on several occasions. They were asked about their experience, their general views on probation practice, and their specific management of the case under consideration. Almost without exception, social workers agreed to the taping and transcription of interviews, and the examination of case records.

In view of their varied background experience, and the need to tailor social work intervention to the needs of each probationer, considerable variation in the content and pattern of supervision was to be expected, and this will be discussed in the next chapter. What was more worrying however, was the lack of any conformity in the basic level of service probationers received. In this chapter therefore, we look at a number of aspects of basic service provision and the variation in existing practice revealed, and consider how far the basic level of service to probationers was satisfactory, in terms of the guidelines laid down and already referred to in chapter 2.

4.1.1 The priority or probation in generic departments

The rationale behind the creation of generic social work departments in Scotland in 1968 was to have one 'open door' through which all clients could have access to social work services. While this has had undoubted advantages in many respects, some drawbacks have become very apparent, one of which is the conflicting claims made by the various client groups on finite social work resources. According to everyone we interviewed, in recent years the main priority of all social work departments has been child care work. Social workers at every level stressed the primary importance placed on child care cases, and acknowledged the implications this had for probation work, which was generally regarded as being of low priority. As one social worker said:

> The main priorities are child care and ensuring that children are not at risk. Probation has come a very very poor probably third, fourth or fifth, I don't know. I suppose quite a long way down.

While it appeared that the statutory element in probation did ensure some degree of priority, there was frequently the implication that this was minimal:

> Probation is a statutory piece of work and it has to be done - in some fashion.

The difficulty of having to supervise probation cases in what was effectively regarded by many workers as a child care department, was manifested at various levels. For instance, there were complaints about insufficient time to supervise probationers properly, or to attend court:

> I was more or less told by my senior, you just cannot spend time on that girl. Give her half an hour and get her out. Just do what you have to do to comply with the order.

The emergency work involved in child care also interfered with regular management of probation cases:

> Child care cases are the most difficult to plan because there's always things happening. And you've very often to leave aside other work you've planned. in order to attend to them, because they are things that won't wait.

Again:

> I had arranged to see the probationer last week, but unfortunately I had an emergency case with a child who had to get received into care, so I had to cancel at the last minute.

Social workers frequently commented that in-service training concentrated on child care at the expense of probation. They also made the point that probation cases were given little attention in individual supervision sessions with senior social workers:

> My own experience of supervision is that you rarely get round to discussing your offender cases. You spend all the time with child care and the elderly at risk.

The priority given to individual probation cases appeared to depend very much on the perceived needs of the case rather than its probation requirements. This influenced the level of service at all levels. If, for example, a case involved a family with a child at risk, it would get priority in allocation, in the social worker's workload and in supervision sessions. However, concentration on the child care aspects often meant that the probation component was bypassed as a result. One such case:

> has not just been talked about between myself and the senior, it has been talked about on an inter-disciplinary level and at area manager level. [Q. Was that relating to the children, or was there a chance to discuss A's probation as well?] I don't think the probation was discussed at all to be honest, because as I say, we were so much involved with the family in other statutory orders.

4.2 Organising a probation order

4.2.1 Relationship with the court

As we saw in chapter 2, considerable variation typified the way social work service to the courts was organised, the formal links between courts and social work departments, and the individual contact between social workers and courts in different areas. Although some variation could be explained by differences in the training, interest and experience of social workers, in general individual links were more in evidence in the small courts, than in the large one with many sheriffs and an extremely large catchment area. In the latter situation it was undoubtedly more difficult to build up personal links for a number of reasons, including lack of time, and nervousness and uncertainty due to unfamiliarity with legal and court procedures. We were told by one worker who had a probationer going to court:

> It would be open for discussion with my senior as to whether I was going to be allocated time to go. I would have to justify why I feel it would be important for me to be there.

And another experienced worker commented:

> Young workers are not comfortable with dealing with the courts. They are nervous about going into court. They are nervous about seeing sheriffs. They are not familiar with procedures, and if you're not familiar with your own procedures and with the court set-up, then you are disconcerted.

Nevertheless, even in the large court some social workers did have direct personal contact with sheriffs when necessary, and demonstrated sound knowledge and confidence in carrying out court based work. Most were older, experienced workers, with a background in the old probation departments, where they had originally forged their links with the court:

> In the old days every probation officer had a fairly close relationship with the court and the sheriffs...you'd go up and you could ask for an appointment and have a tête-à-tête with most sheriffs. Most of them were very co-operative and very glad to see you.

We did however find a few younger workers, with a particular interest in working with offenders, and a certain self confidence, who had also established direct links with sheriffs. As one explained:

> The kind of cookie probationers I've got, I go and speak to the sheriff if I can. It's very straightforward, but most social workers don't use it. I'm surprised they don't because most sheriffs don't know how to deal with odd offences or sexual offenders or inadequate offenders. They are very puzzled about what's the best approach.

Where regular links like these had been established, the relationship was usually two-way and dynamic, with mutual exchange of views which worked to the benefit of the probationer.

4.2.2 Reports and recommendations

In preparing a social enquiry report, a social worker is expected to provide background information to assist the court in passing sentence. The standard text on probation in Scotland (Moore and Wood 1981, p. 62) suggests that:

> There is no obligation to offer any opinion. A good social enquiry report as such assists the sentencing process. Report writers could usefully acknowledge in their reports that 'the sentencing decision is one for the court'. The use of the word 'recommend' (or 'recommendation') in a report tends to suggest the reverse.

Given this statement it is not surprising that social workers at all levels differed widely in their views about making a recommendation, and about what official policy was. Some believed no recommendation at all should be made. Some thought an indication about the suitability of probation might be given, but no other disposal recommended. Others had no qualms about recommending alternative disposals, including fines and custodial sentences, although these tended to be experienced workers with good court links.

Even social workers who thought they shouldn't make recommendations, said they usually did so because it was expected by both colleagues and the courts. Workers admitted that they often attempted to resolve this conflict by resorting to 'negative recommendations' as in the following case:

When I was at college, the lecturer used to write on the blackboard every week 'Thou shalt not recommend'. That was okay in college, but when you came out in the area team, people were aghast that you weren't going to recommend. So I do not recommend because that's stuck in my mind. But what I will do is look at what is available to the court and say perhaps why it wouldn't work.

While most workers said they would base probation recommendations on the needs of the case and the motivation of the offender, it was clear that other factors played a part. While no social workers admitted doing it themselves, there was recognition that other workers sometimes avoided recommending probation as a way of controlling their workload, and that this tendency could be encouraged by higher management:

Although people have not said 'don't recommend probation', they have asked that we consider very carefully for whom we consider probation, because the amount of work we have is hard enough to cope with.

Expressions of unwillingness to operate in this way appeared to confirm the practice:

I think that would be almost criminal. I have heard certain individuals say things like that, 'I'm not going to recommend probation because I'm up to my eyes in it'. I couldn't go along with that. If workers are overworked...then somebody should be looking at their workloads.

On the other hand, where workloads were heavy, there were occasions when a probation recommendation was made in order to try and ensure that a case, which might normally only be seen on an intake basis, would be allocated to a specific social worker to receive ongoing help and a share of scant resources.

Social workers also commented that willingness to recommend probation also related to length of experience, although this too worked both ways. Some experienced workers said they recommended probation less because they were more realistic (or cynical) about the chances of success. Others were more likely to recommend because they felt they had the confidence to tackle more difficult cases, had an awareness of what probation could offer, and enjoyed the confidence of sheriffs, who were consequently more likely to follow their recommendations.

For some social workers, probation recommendations were limited by the identification of clear casework objectives, which would reduce the likelihood of re-offending. Others took a much broader view, including cases where the worker would have a more superficial monitoring role, and thus recommended much more frequently. Another influential factor was the social worker's perception of other disposals. Some who were able to see value in a custodial sentence might recommend it; others, who viewed imprisonment with horror, would recommend probation in order to avoid it, while acknowledging that the chances of success with the probationer were slim.

4.2.3 Allocation of probation work

Client referrals, whether for a court report, supervision of a probation order, or any other kind of social work intervention, are passed to social workers by their senior worker through an allocation system. The social workers interviewed described a number of different ways of allocating cases, the timing and method of which appeared to have a significant effect on the subsequent level of service to probationers. At one extreme, for example, cases were allocated on a rota or random basis, regardless of social work interest or previous contact with the case:

> It's done on a rota basis, so if it's your turn to do an SER you do it...you might have been working with the family for a long time, but someone else will pick it up.

This method caused considerable frustration to workers, because they felt their interests and abilities had not been taken into account, and that they were obliged to tackle work in which they had insufficient expertise or experience, resulting in a poorer service to the probationer.

At the other extreme, and just as unsatisfactory from the worker's point of view, were the informal and 'democratic' team allocation meetings, where workers volunteered for the cases they were interested in. This was followed by a process of negotiation, which team members considered inefficient and time wasting, with 'unpopular' cases being left unallocated:

> We had a meeting where, basically, the senior would give information about what was on offer, and I suppose it was like a game of cards. You know, people would say 'I've got room for that', or 'I'll take that', and eventually you would feel 'well it's my turn and I'll have to take something'.

Two intermediate types of allocation were thought to work well and efficiently, allowing workers to specialise to a limited extent, thereby building up a pool of shared knowledge and expertise within the team. In the first, the senior allocated cases directly, according to the worker's special skills and interests. In the second, allocation meetings were held, with the senior allocating cases, but allowing room for discussion and exchange:

> In the last allocation meeting we had, I was asked to take a case I didn't want, but I took it nonetheless. But later on in the meeting another social worker was imposed with a case they didn't want but took anyway. So I

said 'why don't we swop over because I'm much more interested in that', and he said 'that's great'.

It might be assumed that once an offender had been allocated to a social worker for a social enquiry report, the same social worker would continue to supervise the probationer should an order be made. In fact, it might be returned to another worker through the allocation system. In the cases we examined this happened for a number or reasons.

First, a case was sometimes allocated in order to provide a more appropriate service to a probationer, for example, where a female worker had completed the report and it was thought a male supervisor would be more suitable. More often however, it seemed to be just a matter of policy, and this could create difficulties for the offender:

> That particular one ended up assuming I was the social worker and that was very awkward because I had to explain to him that he would be allocated another social worker. I had visited him in prison and he knew I had been quite understanding. He's a bit put out.

Re-allocation at this stage could often lead to delays in probationers receiving service, a particularly undesirable consequence in the light of the general feeling that 'it's important to strike while the iron is hot'. Whereas the guidelines stated that 'all probation orders should be allocated within the first week of their receipt by a social work office', case records showed that over a third of allocations failed to meet this standard. As many as 21 cases were not allocated for at least two weeks after disposal, eight were still unallocated after several months, and one three year order remained unallocated for two and a half years. Many workers confirmed that by the time a new order had been brought into the allocation system (and a worker found who had space to take on the supervision) a considerable gap could occur.

It is interesting to note that such cases were not regarded by management as unallocated, but 'allocated upwards'. This meant that if no basic grade worker was available to supervise the probationer, it was formally held by the senior social worker, or sometimes the area manager. While, technically, this may have satisfied the minimal requirements of the order, in practice it meant that no work was done with the probationer during that time. It appeared that in some extreme cases, probation orders had effectively been 'unallocated' in this way for the entire length of the order. One senior social worker who had just taken over an area team, described the practice which apparently existed in a number of area offices.

> When I came here there were a significant number of cases in what was called the centrally held file. Basically that was a fancy term for unallocated cases. That has been the pattern, as far as I can see, for a

number of years, and one that was never questioned by management or by the team here.

4.3 Supervising a probation order

4.3.1 Serving the order

Once a probation order is made by the court, it is passed to a named supervising social worker, who is responsible for 'serving' it on the probationer. The guidelines state that 'all probation orders should be served within one week of receipt by the supervising officer' and as we saw earlier, sheriffs also considered prompt, initial contact with the probationer to be important. In practice, case records showed that only 39 of the 84 probationers (we have omitted two who died during the course of the order) had been seen within two weeks of disposal, and 15 had still not been seen after several months. Many of the extreme delays were due to re-allocation after the order was made, but other organisational and administrative factors also played a part:

> I would always attempt to serve the order within seven days of it being made. That is complicated by the fact that the mail system in this office is absolutely chaotic and you're quite likely not to get the order for weeks. But normally if we don't get it through the mail here, we'll phone the sheriff clerk and go down and collect another copy, and at least serve the order and explain what's involved in probation.

While many social workers waited until the piece of paper arrived to serve the order, good direct links with the court could expedite the process, sometimes allowing the order to be served the same day:

> The sheriff court generally phones me up to let me know that somebody's been placed on probation and wants to make a first appointment, and I generally say that afternoon, if I'm in that afternoon, and they come down.

The regional guidelines already referred to state that 'the precise terms and conditions of the order must be clearly explained at the time together with consequences of non-compliance and further offending'. All the social workers interviewed said they did this in the first meeting with the probationer and many stressed that this set the tone for the whole probation process:

> The first interview with them is important in that you spell out why and what sort of aims we have got, what steps I would take if they don't comply, and make it clear that it is not just an idle threat.

One social worker explained how important it was to stress immediately the general conditions of an order: to be of good behaviour, to conform to the directions of the social worker and to notify changes of address or employment:

> If you really lay the guidelines down clearly at the beginning, you are less likely to breach people...If you're nebulous and a wee bit airy-fairy, a lot of people sense that and think probation isn't worth while.

As an indication that they have understood and agreed with the conditions of the order, the guidelines state 'the order should be signed by the probationer and then countersigned by the supervising officer'. In fact practice varied considerably; some orders were not signed at all, some were signed only by the probationer, others were signed by both. Social workers who liked both parties to sign often used it to create a two-way commitment. As one said:

> I always make it very clear that these requirements are set down by the sheriff court, not by the supervising officer. I like to make it clear these are conditions of the order. 'They're binding on you and they're binding on me. And if you don't comply with these conditions, this is what I have to do'.

Another experienced worker saw it as something which could also be used later on as part of the probation process:

> If you're reviewing their probation, or you've got concerns that they're going to go out there and blow it, then it's sometimes useful to say, 'look you remember that document we signed? That's still important, that's still got a long way to run. Let's have a look at it again. Let's see what you agreed to on that day '. And that can be effective.

All social workers also said they used the first interview to assess with the probationer what probation might offer, but this was done at different levels of generality depending on the view of probation held by the social worker. Some confined it to a general offer of help if needed, some set goals for the probationer which varied from the very general to the very specific. Others used it to form a contract with the probationer on work to be done during the probation period.

Not all workers waited till the order was granted to explain conditions and negotiate goals. Some saw it as part of the preparation for the court report either because help was urgently needed or as an aid to assessment of the suitability of probation:

> My own personal way of working would be that you would already be indicating areas and checking out with them whether they would see this as being an area of their life that would benefit from further advice and

51

guidance. You would be explaining in great detail the statutory requirement of a probation order and gauging whether they recognised that, and would be able to give a commitment to it. So all of that would be done even before you actually get to the point of a court making a probation order.

4.3.2 Frequency of contact

Once an order had been served, the guidelines specify a minimum of five contacts with the probationer in the first three months of the order (i.e. approximately every three weeks) and thereafter a minimum of monthly contact. As we saw in chapter 2, most sheriffs who specified minimum expectations of contact set them more frequently during the initial months, tailing off if appropriate thereafter. Although most social workers agreed that they tried to adhere to this standard, they admitted that, in practice, contacts were often much less frequent, a view confirmed by analysis of case records. In fact only 43 of the 84 cases were seen as often as thrice weekly in the first few months of the order with seven cases not seen at all during that time.

The reasons for this were depressingly familiar: delays in allocation or re-allocation, or cases being nominally allocated to a senior social worker, and seen on a intake basis only if the probationer requested help with a specific problem. Many probationers were irregular attenders, appointments were missed and there were delays in making new ones. Sometimes probation appointments were missed by social workers, due to crises, mainly in child care cases. We found too that it was not always possible for social workers to use their own discretion in relation to the frequency with which they saw probationers. In one case, for example, a social worker told us:

> I've been to see her about three times in hospital. I feel I should be going once a week but my senior management doesn't allow that. I've been told that once in three weeks is enough.

Finally some lengthy gaps occurred due to transfer of cases from one social worker to another. For many of the probationers changes of social worker were just a fact of life. Almost half had experienced at least one change during their order (excluding re-allocation between the social enquiry report and serving of the order) with 12 having two or three changes, and one having five, only one of which was due to a change of residence by the probationer. It was clear that many probationers experienced disrupted supervision in the course of their order. Some of these were unavoidable, as when a probationer moved area, a student left placement, or a worker fell ill or was promoted. Others however appeared to be due to administrative changes which, whatever the perceived organisational advantages, did little for the probationers or social workers concerned:

> The restructuring started last November, and it's been trickling on ever since. It's a nightmare, it really is. In the long run it might be of benefit, but it's very difficult to see where the benefits are. They're sort of lost in here.

As well as disruption to the supervision process, changes of social worker sometimes resulted in serious interruptions in frequency of contact because of delay in transfer. Case records showed that ten of the 84 cases were recorded as unallocated to any supervising social worker for periods of several months during the order. In two cases they were unallocated for over a year, and while one of these was technically allocated to a senior social worker he was not seen at all during that time.

4.3.3 Additional requirements

In addition to the general requirements of a probation order, courts may impose additional ones, which may be either mandatory or 'at the discretion of the supervising officer'. We encountered 20 such cases, mainly necessitating attendance at psychiatric hospitals or clinics, and drug or alcohol rehabilitation units.

In most cases there was little communication or planning between the social worker and the specialist agency. Usually the two worked entire separately, with an occasional telephone call from the social worker to check on progress. In a small number of cases, this meant that the probationer fell between two stools. In one such case, the social worker regarded the probationer's condition of residence at a hostel as releasing him from the need for any contact once the order had been served, believing that the hostel staff were responsible for supervision. In another instance, a similar view was taken by the specialist agency, and the probationer was effectively discharged without any treatment.

While social workers generally regarded additional requirements as helpful, and indeed often requested them, in practice they presented a number of difficulties. Problems of communication have been mentioned above, but perhaps even more important was the difference in philosophy, leading to a potential conflict of goals, and differential response to the probationer's behaviour. For example, a requirement to attend a centre which works on the basis of voluntary attendance, such as Alcoholics Anonymous, can cause problems for both the agency and the social worker if the probationer fails to attend, or continues sporadically to abuse drink or drugs. This may be regarded as part of the essential rehabilitation process by the centre, but seen as grounds for breaching the order by the social worker.

Problems of confidentiality could also occur in this situation. Should the social worker be notified if the probationer continued to abuse? Does fear of this inhibit the probationer from confiding in centre staff? What happens if the order is going well generally, but the probationer is failing to meet a special requirement and, if reported to the court, faces the possibility of custody. Case records revealed two cases of this kind where clear failure to comply with an additional requirement was being ignored by the social worker for this reason.

4.4 Ending a probation order

4.4.1 Early discharge

Although a probation order is made for a fixed period, it is open to both social worker and probationer to apply to the court for the order to be discharged early. In fact it is suggested in the guidelines that this 'should be actively considered if no further benefit is to be accrued' from continuing the order. Some social workers however saw early discharge in a more positive light and actively encouraged it:

> The effect it has on the probationer is a massive boost to their confidence. and I enjoy doing it. I get a lot of satisfaction from doing it.

This worker estimated that she applied for early discharge in about a third of cases, but was certainly untypical in this. Although many other workers supported the idea in theory, in only three cases had an application been made. A number of reasons were given for this. One worker did not know that it was possible, 'to be quite honest I didn't know the option was there'.

Several were willing but said they did not know the procedures and had no time to check them out:

> I thought it would probably be appropriate and to be absolutely honest the only reason I didn't pursue it is that I haven't even had the time and I really would have to read up how to go about it.

Other social workers thought sheriffs were against it particularly where the order had not been running smoothly and further offences had been committed:

> The courts are very unhappy about terminating probation early if further offences have been committed. That is the experience in this office...because I have tried on numerous occasions to terminate the probation of someone when the court is aware that they have committed a further offence, and the court has declined to terminate.

Elsewhere the sheer time taken by discharge procedures coupled with the belief that the sheriff might not agree anyway persuaded some workers not to even initiate the procedure, particularly towards the end of an order. In this case it was easier to space out contact than go through the necessary formalities of termination:

> It is one of these cases that are 'riding out'. Now that's an unfortunate phrase but it means that you just monitor things to keep it ticking over. You do the bare minimum... I know it should be terminated early, but I haven't done that because it was up in a couple of months and I feel there is no point in taking it back to court at this late stage.

Another social worker, in similar circumstances, told us:

> I think the difficulty is procedural, it takes a number of months. If you have gone maybe six months it can take you a further two or three months to get the thing through court, getting it up there and getting it discharged and various things. Many people don't bother.

It can also happen that a social worker is keen to discharge the order early but the probationer refuses because of the support they feel they are getting. One social worker told us ruefully that 'one or two people I considered it with, where I actually wanted early termination, wanted to keep it on'.

4.4.2 Breaching

A conviction for a further offence after a probation order has been made, automatically constitutes a breach of probation as does non-compliance with the requirements of the order. In these circumstances the social worker has a duty to report back to the court, though he may ask for the order to be continued. Following a breach the probationer may be sentenced for the original offence as well as any further offence that has been committed.

The guidelines state that 'the conviction of all offences committed since a probation order has been issued must be formally reported to the court without delay'. This was not merely a matter of departmental policy, but a statutory duty. Nevertheless we found considerable variation and not a small amount of confusion among social workers on this issue.

In the first place, many workers experienced conflict between their natural and professional inclination to support the client, and their equally professional duty to the court. They did not find the words of the guidelines that 'care and supervision...are complementary rather than being mutually exclusive' an easy alliance. In the view of one senior social worker in a team where several workers were supervising probation cases:

> It's a very far reaching thing to do to breach someone's probation. They will probably end up with a period in prison...very few cases you breach won't end up like that. Within probation there's a very, very strong

authority element. In terms of the training the social worker has received, and the role they play for most of their working day, it doesn't rest easy with them. It goes against their general philosophy of work practice.

At one extreme however, we found social workers who were able to use the authority inherent in the order in a positive manner, maintaining a policy of informing the court as soon as they knew there was a further charge pending:

> I always notify a breach if there's another offence, although I may often say I would like the order to continue...If the probationer tells me he has been picked up at the weekend for house breaking, I will check with the fiscal when the case is likely to come to court if he knows, and then notify a breach of probation as soon as possible...I think it gives the sheriffs more confidence in the use of probation if they know you are keeping on top of the offences

At the other extreme there was clear evidence from case notes that, in five cases, further offences had not been reported, and there were indications from interviews with probationers of a further two cases of this kind. Social workers too, were well aware that this sometimes happened, giving as reasons, 'pressure of work', 'not worth proceeding with, because of the time factor', and in one instance (following a further conviction) failure to breach because the social worker thought the offender was innocent! In all of these instances however, and despite the reasons given, the failure to breach appeared to have as much to do with the worker's general view of probation, as with the circumstances of the actual offence.

In terms of the requirement for the probationer to comply with the conditions of the order, the guidelines insisted that 'supervising workers must not condone the client's failure to comply'. The somewhat vague wording of this edict realistically reflected the practice situation, where workers had considerable discretion in deciding what constituted non-compliance. The uncertainty and varying opinions about this could lead to very uneven practice as our investigations showed.

One general requirement of a probation order, for example, is that the probationer must inform the supervising officer of any change in residence or employment. Although this appears to be an unambiguous statement, social workers varied considerably in breaching on this ground. In a number of cases we were attempting to follow through, the whereabouts of the probationers were not known and no action had been taken, sometimes for several months. In contrast where a probationer's disappearance was taken seriously as a failure to comply, breach procedures were sometimes taken within a matter of days.

In a situation where social workers must have some discretion about what constitutes non-compliance, where possible grounds for breaching are many and varied, and where most social workers tend to give the probationer the benefit of the doubt - at least initially - it is difficult to define where discretion ends and condonation begins. Taking the most lenient view possible however, case records still showed nine cases where a significant breach of the requirements had not been reported.

Social workers identified a number of factors which led to a reluctance to breach. First was the need to obtain adequate evidence:

> It is important to try and prove a breach of the probation order...you've got to get evidence, and corroborated evidence, for that. In fact I think some of the procurators fiscal are saying that we need to be quite clear that, if it's not a commission of a further offence, we need to consult with them before we breach people just now, because of the number of ones that have been thrown out.

Difficulties could also be created if the probationer was breached on grounds of non-compliance and probation continued against the recommendation of the social worker. Whereas for some offenders it did provide a timely reminder of their situation, improving motivation, for other probationers and their supervisors continuing supervision seemed fairly pointless. The fear of this happening certainly made some social workers reluctant to breach.

The discretion associated with defining non-compliance and reporting a breach on those grounds was experienced as a heavy responsibility by many younger, inexperienced workers. It was less of a burden to older, more experienced supervisors, especially those with a background or special interest in probation. They saw themselves much more clearly as acting on the court's authority, and thus felt less personal responsibility and discomfort, as shown in the following quote:

> I see my job as an extension of the court, so you have a duty. I dislike doing it, particularly the one I was saying I breached a few months ago because she was refusing to keep appointments. Only had about two months to go and it was absolutely stupid on her part. But I had no choice, having made four appointments to see her and she didn't keep them. I had no choice but to do it.

Whereas some social workers regarded breaching a probationer as 'the end of the line' and a reflection of their inability to offer appropriate help, others saw it as part of the ongoing process of supervision; a positive tool that could be used to assist the probationer. They therefore breached more readily, often recommending that probation should continue and confident that sheriffs would be likely to so recommend.

The question of breaching raises the question of who the probation 'contract' is between. Two views were evident among social workers; the first that the primary contract was between the worker and the probationer; the second that the contract was between the court and the offender, formalised at the time the probationer agreed to the order being made.

The first stance gave rise to dilemmas when the probationer was doing well in casework terms, but failing to meet formal requirements which the social worker regarded as unimportant. These were then ignored either as peripheral issues, or because they were seen as personal rather than statutory shortcomings:

> He needs a lot of help, he really does. Then just as I was helping him, he doesn't even bother to let me know he's gone back to work, or that he's failed to keep his appointments.

From the second perspective, failures to meet requirements were taken very seriously, with the social worker having no alternative but to go back to the court. Often workers found sheriffs sympathetic to their aims in these situations and were able to enlist the court's support and authority in their work with the probationer:

> I had an 18 year old who was continually shifting about from one place to another, would get employment, have a steady address, then get involved in something else and end up in remand. Then we would see her again, although the contact was sporadic because you never quite knew where to find her. The court was actually good with that, because they understood the circumstances, and the young person who was homeless, not terribly bright, made some effort, did show some commitment, didn't disappear entirely and would always show up eventually.

In several instances social workers said they were reluctant to breach because they thought the social work department itself had contributed to the non-compliance through organisational confusion and delay. In one reported case, for example:

> I had one young man who was on probation and it was all very messy, because it didn't get transferred to us and there was a long gap before I picked it up...and it was very unsatisfactory because he never turned up when he was supposed to. I could never find him in the house. It was only about four months to the end of his order so I just kept it till then. I didn't breach him because the social work department had made such a mess of things that I felt we were on pretty sticky ground if we then started, you know, as we'd left it about six months without allocating it.

This was not always the perceived rationale however. In another case which had been unallocated for a considerable period, the worker to whom it was finally assigned moved swiftly into breach proceedings when the probationer failed to attend for appointments as requested. In this case he felt that he had to 'cover himself' precisely because of the failure of the department earlier on.

Finally the degree of sympathy a social worker feels for a probationer influences the decision whether to breach. Sometimes this works to the advantage of the client, but certainly not always. In one instance for example, when a social worker had little personal contact with a probationer, but thought he was being 'taken for a ride' he instituted breach proceedings remarkably swiftly. In another case where he knew the probationer well and admitted he had a good deal of sympathy with her circumstances, he was much more reluctant to breach.

It is clear that the issues raised by breaching are many and complex, and certainly they caused difficulties and dilemmas for many of the social workers we interviewed. Their resolution depended as much on the worker's attitude towards probation in general as on the circumstances of individual cases. We shall examine this in more detail in the next chapter.

4.5 Level of service

We have already indicated that probation practice often fell short of the standards set by the guidelines on a number of important dimensions. In 84 of the cases studied we were able, through analysis of case records, to combine these dimensions, distilling four clear categories of basic service received by probationers. The remainder of the cases had to be excluded mainly because of insufficient information. In one instance case records were unavailable, and in another the probationer refused access.

Seventeen of the cases reached what we termed a 'satisfactory' service. In this category probationers were allocated to a social worker within one week of the order being made; were first seen within two weeks of the disposal, and thereafter a minimum of once every three weeks for the first few months. Furthermore, there were no changes of social worker, except where a probationer had moved, and no periods of non-allocation. Finally, breaches were not condoned, and case records specified clearly the type and frequency of contact.

A further 29 probationers received a 'reasonable' service: the case allocated within one month of disposal; the first meeting with the social worker within six weeks of the order being made, and thereafter a meeting at least once monthly for the first few months. There was no more than one change of social worker per year of order. Again breaches were not condoned, and frequency and type of contact was recorded.

Service was assessed as 'poor' (27 cases) if it fell below the 'reasonable' standards in one or more aspects, and as 'very poor' (12 cases) if the fall in standards was rated extreme by two researchers independently. In practice such cases stood out very clearly, as the following examples show:

Case A. Case A was an adult recidivist, on a three year order, because he was thought to be 'at a turning point' and in need of support and encouragement. He was seen three times in the first five months, then his social worker was promoted and left the office. The case was then effectively unallocated for the next 16 months (although technically it was regarded as 'allocated upwards' to the senior social worker). During this period no attempt was made to contact the probationer. Finally a new social worker was given the case. She attempted to get in touch with the probationer, but he had moved away. His ex-cohabitee said he had been under the impression his probation had ended. After several attempts to trace him had failed, he was breached for failing to inform of change of address. A warrant was issued for his arrest, but police attempts to trace him also failed.

Case B. Case B was a first offender, pregnant with one older child. She had a long history of drug abuse, and was the subject of an 18 month order for a drugs offence, with a requirement to refrain from controlled drugs and to attend a specialist clinic. The case was unallocated for nearly three months and then given to a student social worker on a practice placement in the agency, as an emergency referral from the maternity hospital, after the probationer had been admitted antenatally for detoxification. She was seen regularly for two months, when the student's leaving summary noted, 'due to the fact that she is on 18 months probation, her drug abuse, and the risk to the unborn child, I recommend that this case be re-allocated'. Instead it was returned to the 'central file' (effectively unallocated). A month later there was a further emergency referral from the hospital, and this time the case was allocated to a social worker as a 'child at risk' case. As such the case received frequent monitoring over the next few months, both by the social worker and at more senior management level. However, despite substantial and substantiated evidence that the probationer was continuing to abuse drugs, and not attending the clinic, she was not breached as it was feared this would result in custody. Eventually her non-compliance was discovered by a sheriff who became involved in the child care aspects of the case, and who insisted that she was breached. This was done, and contrary to the fears of the social worker, probation was continued, after a recommendation to that effect, and finally completed.

4.5.1 Summary

In general, the level of service was considerably higher in the smaller court areas, where 12 of the 42 cases analysed received satisfactory service, a further 22 received reasonable service, and there were none which were very poor (and only 9 which were poor). In contrast, the level of service in the large court area was much lower, with only 12 of the 42 cases analysed meeting the 'satisfactory' or 'reasonable' standard, and 30 probationers receiving a poor or very poor service. It was noticeable too, that nearly all the 'reasonable' and 'satisfactory' cases were located in three offices in suburban areas on the edge of the city; offices where social workers considered that pressures of work, particularly in child care, were lower than average. The data assembled therefore, certainly seemed to confirm the view of social workers, that probation cases were not high priority, especially when faced with the competition of high child care loads.

5 Intervention approaches

5.1 Background

As already stated, the variations in practice noted in the previous chapter can partly be explained by the needs of particular cases, but are also greatly influenced by the supervisor's general orientation towards probation. As the court has discretion in the use of probation as a disposal, so the supervising social worker may select from a variety of methods and resources in working with the probationer. To some extent the choice of level and style of intervention will depend on a personal interpretation of such concepts as guidance, treatment, supervision and assistance, as well as the relative importance placed on each of these various elements.

Hardiker (1977) and Hardiker and Webb (1979) have presented interesting findings related to social work ideologies and practice. In a small scale in depth study of English probation officers' social enquiry practices they found that, in a self administered questionnaire, some officers tended to profess more of a treatment orientation than others, and that this difference was related to length of experience, type of training, and whether or not the officer was a graduate.

What was especially interesting though, was that, whatever the probation officer's stated general ideology, in discussion of individual cases every one held a treatment orientation towards at least some cases. Moreover there was no association between orientations in the self administered scales and those in the interview cases. The researchers concluded that a number of factors influenced treatment preferences in practice, including the severity of the offence, the personal characteristics of the offender, family circumstances, and the extent and nature of previous convictions. In short, operational ideologies were 'mediated by the exigencies of practice'.

At root of many of the problems experienced by probation officers in England and Wales, and social workers supervising probation orders in Scotland is the need to work simultaneously within judicial and social work frameworks, with their differing underlying ideologies and different demands. One of the main functions of the former is to act as an advisor in decision making to the court, through the preparation of social enquiry reports. In the latter the main emphasis is on helping the offender with his problems as part of the rehabilitative process (Monger, 1972).

This potential conflict between 'care' and 'control' in probation work runs deep enough to have been noted by many who have studied probation (Titmus, 1954; Parsloe, 1967; Fielding, 1984; and Celnick, 1985). There have been practical attempts to resolve the problem, and these, too, have been examined. Celnick, for example, studied an area team's attempt to carry out probation supervision, based on a non-treatment paradigm of standardised practice developed by Bottoms and McWilliams (1979). The team attempted to remove the core ambiguity of the traditional 'casework' approach to supervision by adopting instead a contract reporting system. This, Celnick concluded, only served to obscure the conflict, leading to 'legalistic arguments to justify failure to abide by the rules, or else open admittance that the aim of helping clients took precedence over enforcing the order'.

In the traditional approach, it is suggested, an acceptable balance is achieved by rationalising that 'care' helps the offender to 'control' his behaviour. In this way, role conflict can be submerged, and the worker can fulfil responsibilities without making difficult choices between the two. Yet, whether one considers the choices made in the project described by Celnick, or examines studies of the more traditional approach, in the great majority of cases it is, in practice, the perceived need of the individual probationer which is paramount (Lawson 1978; and Fielding, 1986).

The non-treatment paradigm developed by Bottoms and McWilliams (1979) does assist in developing ideas about probation supervision beyond the purely 'casework' approach. It identifies four basic aims of practice under which all other objectives can be assumed. These are: the provision of appropriate help for offenders; the statutory supervision of offenders; diverting appropriate offenders from custodial sentences; and, more generally, the reduction of crime.

However, social workers in the area team studied by Celnick, found that in practice identification of these elements itself posed further problems. They were unclear about the difference between 'treatment' and 'help' and had an inadequate conceptualisation of the latter. Some found it difficult to distinguish between what they termed 'personal' and 'professional' help, or to define 'appropriate' help in any given circumstances. Others demonstrated uncertainties about the rules and boundaries of statutory supervision, and even those who were clear about them in a strictly legal sense, interpreted them differently.

The idea of 'appropriate help' has attracted the attention of a number of researchers. For Bottoms and McWilliams (1979), it includes anything that is neither illegal or immoral; for Sainsbury (1982), it is help that is directed towards change in the individual or his circumstances; and for Davies (1981) it is that obligations both to the state and the client have to be recognised. If 'help' rather than 'treatment' is to be a useful basis for probation supervision then practitioners need to be clear about the range of activities which are allowable for them, and where the boundaries and limits lie.

One way to achieve a mutually acceptable compatibility between care and control was suggested by the Development Sub Committee of Region 7 of the Chief Probation Officer's Conference (1978). It proposed a primary contract with the court which would stipulate the frequency with which the probationer should report to his supervisor, and suggested that such a contract would both 'limit the discretion which probation officers have exercised idiosyncratically', and emphasise the binding nature of the legal aspect of probation.

The control elements of supervision would be satisfied by the primary contract, leaving the supervisor and probationer free to make a secondary contract for social work help where the desire for this is indicated by the probationer. This approach rejects the idea of the social worker as a treatment agent, diagnosing the problem and instituting a course of action in the best interest of the client. Instead it frees him to respond to any difficulties the probationer wishes to discuss, and places on him the responsibility to provide opportunities for assistance of all kinds.

Several schemes based on this approach have been both tried and studied (Coker, 1982; Hil, 1982) and, although these vary in some respects, the initial response from courts, probationers and supervisors has been favourable. Hil's study, in particular, highlights explicitly the importance of conceptual images in practice, drawing specific attention to the clients' perceptions of probation practice.

The debate about 'treatment' and 'help' models of intervention is useful in that it places increased emphasis on client defined problems and needs, a shift in attention that has been reflected in a number of studies (Parker, 1974; Davies, 1979; Sainsbury, 1982). One of the main findings to emerge is the differing perception of probationers and supervisors in relation to both the theory and practice of probation, particularly in the case of traditional one-to-one office based interviews (Davies, 1981). Thus, as Hil notes, while probation supervisors may see their work as helpful and client centred, clients themselves may well take the opposite view and argue that supervisors are mainly concerned with control, punishment and surveillance.

As Hil's study of a probation day centre suggests, the wider range and different forms of assistance envisaged in the 'help' approach may well change probationers' perception of probation. In this study, not only did probationers' perceptions of day care differ from their view of traditional supervision, but there was far greater agreement between probationers and supervisors about the elements of supervision and their relative importance.

Hil describes how, in an effort to clarify probationers' perceptions of the service provided at the centre, nine possible elements of supervision were identified and clearly defined. These were: punishment, retribution, control, containment, treatment, help, care, friendship and companionship. Probationers and supervisors were then asked to list them in descending order of importance. There was sufficient agreement between the two groups to distil three main categories, each containing two or more elements. Priority was given to a 'help-care' orientation, encompassing the elements of help, care, friendship and companionship. Next came a 'soft control' approach embracing notions of control and containment, with a 'hard control' line based on punishment and retribution being given very low ranking. Treatment was not considered to be a significant element by either group.

5.2 Intervention approaches in Scotland

In order to examine more closely the content of social work intervention we analysed our taped interviews with probationers and social workers, and carefully examined case records. From the data we were able to draw up a number of broad approaches to the social work supervision of probationers.

There was a high degree of coincidence between the accounts of intervention obtained from all three sources. Of the 43 cases where probationers were interviewed, only nine showed a difference of perception between probationers and social workers. In these instances, a decision about how to categorise the case was made by two researchers assessing independently. The assessments coincided in all instances. In cases where there was no probationer interview, evidence from the casenotes conflicted with the social worker's perception of supervision in only four cases. Here the approach used was categorised on the written evidence, as this appeared to give the most objective picture. In 15 cases it was not possible to classify the approach as no work had been done with the probationer, either because of non-allocation, immediate breach, or the disappearance of the offender.

The intervention approaches outlined below refer to styles of work and not types of social worker. Social workers did talk of 'general' ways of working with probationers, but, in practice, most varied their approach depending on the circumstances of each case; thus what they said they did 'in general' by no means always coincided with what they did 'in particular'. It should be stressed too, that while in some cases classifying the approach was very straightforward, in others a combination of approaches was more apparent. Nevertheless, in most cases one style of approach was predominant, particularly in areas such as making recommendations, serving the order, the worker's relationship with the court, the content of work, and thereafter, breaching and discharging the order.

5.2.1 Court agent approach

> I think it's important for the person to know what they have to do, and they have to know why you're there. It's very important to say 'it's a probation order'. You might be there to try and help them, but at the same time you're still an officer of the court and cannot condone their offending.

The fundamental characteristic of this approach is the social worker's awareness of the close relationship with the court. This may be personal and dynamic or much more formal, depending on a number of factors. These include external organisational influences such as the size of the court, and the management policy of the social work department; and more personal ones including pressure of work, the knowledge, confidence and skill of the worker, and actual interest in probation supervision. In all cases however the ;'court agent' orientation predominates.

This has important consequences. Within this approach the authority of the social worker is defined as coming from the judicial system; thus there are no qualms about using court-derived power when necessary, as in a breach situation for example. The court's authority also gives the social worker the right and confidence to tackle difficult problem areas, to 'push' the probationer, to confront him when the need arises, and to monitor progress.

In addition, the court's authority provides both a structure and focus for setting specific goals for supervision. While probationers may have the opportunity to consent to or veto these, it is clear that the social worker sets the pace Overall, supervision is carried out within a clearly understood framework of requirements, within which care and control are generally combined without undue conflict, and court authority is seen and used as an aid to effective supervision.

Within this approach three different emphases were apparent; befriending, rehabilitating, and supervising.

Befriending. While social workers see the main purpose of probation as rehabilitation, they take a very broad view of the supervision remit and frequently include contact and activities with the probationer's family. Work also tends to be open ended and often starts from a very practical perspective. It has a strong 'befriending' component and is sometimes imaginative and outreaching with the social worker going well beyond the strict requirements of the order, such as taking children in the family swimming or helping to arrange a family holiday.

In relation to personal problems, concrete goals are set and worked towards, within a framework of general counselling. Although offences may be generally blamed on structural societal deficiencies, the social worker is usually very positive in offering practical advice and assistance in trying to get employment of housing.

While authority is not an explicit element in the supervisory relationship, it provides the context for it and is used if necessary. Probationers who had experienced this style of supervision described their social workers as being 'like a friend' and spoke frequently of the positive quality of the relationship and the amount of practical help received. Although the authority element was not always perceived as important, most probationers knew it was there 'in the background'. Here is a typical reminiscence from a probationer:

> He's got me talking about things I wouldn't have dreamed of talking about. Some of them are shocked what you say to them, but not him. He takes it all quite calm. At Christmas time he took me and the bairns to get Christmas presents...he took my son to the baths...he's helping me mentally because I had no self confidence. He's saying to me 'you can do things'. I can stand and fight for myself now, or speak up, so that's been really good social work. At one point I asked him to take my children away and he says 'you can cope'. I lost all confidence...I didn't think I was mothering them right or anything at all. Mentally he helped me to get back out of the house...he was very, very patient but a wee bit persistent. In a way it's made me independent...thinking back now I think that probation saved my life.

Rehabilitating. This approach is not simply one of task-centred case work applied to probation. Essentially probationers describe social workers using this approach as 'making me want to change'. Social workers themselves see the purpose of their intervention, not simply as the pursuit of diminished of criminal activity, but as changing the probationer's fundamental life-style, mainly in relation to alcohol abuse or delinquent activities and associates.

In contrast to task-centred casework, goals are not mutually determined, but are largely set by the social worker. This is followed by sincere attempts to engage the probationer's commitment to them, within a manifestly caring and helpful relationship. The actual content of supervision tends to be a combination of confrontation, and focused work on identified problems.

Progress is checked by close and consistent monitoring, and lavishly rewarded with psychological 'gold stars'. Probationers who experienced this type of intervention gave vivid pictures of a committed and caring relationship forming the context for 'pushy' confrontational work. As one put it:

> She kept telling me get off my backside and every time I come she asks me again. I found out about things I could do at college, just so that I could come back and let her know that I hadn't been sitting down all the time. She did spur me into action...I've always wanted to do it but I've never. I've missed appointments and that. That's been through my job and I've failed to make new ones. And once she wrote me a letter that you get off a bank manager when you are overdrawn!...you know, warning me if I wasn't willing to comply with the order.... I had to come down and apologise. I mean, she doesn't just see you as a name on a list...she sees you as a person. I had never really thought about how much drink I actually consumed, and actually we started thinking about it. It's ideas, you know, that she puts into your head, that you start thinking about. The way I look at it, it depends if the social worker is determined enough to try and get somebody to help themselves. There is an awful lot of people that if they had a sort of pushy social worker, that really wanted to help them, they could gain from it.

Supervising. This approach is similar to the probationer clinic model described by Coker (1982) and Hil (1982), but is less contractual and more 'outreaching'. The authority context for the relationship is provided by an initial baseline of expectations, set down by the social worker in terms of the basic requirements of the order. However, within that context the relationship is deliberately relaxed and friendly, aimed at building a mutual trust which becomes the background for seeking and giving help.

Supervision is close and consistent, and monitoring far from minimal, with the worker taking active steps to ensure that progress is as reported. Again, probationers who experienced this kind of intervention tended to be very clear about its nature, and positive in their response:

> He has the authority to put me straight back.. he has the authority, but it doesn't seem like that at all. You get a coffee and a smoke and a relax! It is not apparent... I'm not an easy guy to get on with, but if I trust someone I get on with them. He won mine...he's always there for a laugh, he enjoys a good joke. He is more of a mate than anything else well, I see him as a mate. I see friendship which is easier to deal with, rather than laying down rules and me just sitting there. He's no Judas.

5.2.2 Welfare agent approach

> I don't like the social control bit of social work. I don't see myself as a policeman. Had I wanted to be a policeman, I would have been a policeman.

Compared to the 'court agent' approach, this style of supervision stems from a fundamentally different view of the social workers role in terms of the relationship to the court. As far as possible the social worker operates independently of the court, viewing supervision of probationers as another form of·normal non-statutory social work. Many of these workers feel uncomfortable or unhappy about authority as a component of a helping relationship, and see care and control as conflicting.

For 'welfare agents' obligations to the court are denied, evaded or only minimally recognised. The authority given to a social worker by the probation order isn't used, unless it suits the social worker, in which case it is used instrumentally. The probation order is seen only as a convenience for getting a case allocated, for example, or for holding on to a difficult client, but it is not seem as an intrinsic part of the supervisory process. The relationship with the client is primary, and non-probation aspects of the case are paramount.

If client needs conflict with probation requirements, the social worker often mediates between client and court, even to the extent of protecting the client against the court, by not reporting non-compliance or further offences. Actual work with the probationer may be task-centred, intensive or minimal. The essence is that the probation content is seen either as irrelevant or intrusive, and the 'real' work is between social worker and client. This approach comes in two guises; pro-active and reactive.

Pro-active. The pro-active 'welfare agent' has clear goals of his own for the case, which may or may not be made explicit to the probationer. In such cases, social workers may work in quite a focused, task-centred way on the case, but the statutory framework of the order is mostly ignored.

In the cases we examined the pro-active welfare approach was often present where a mother has been put on probation. Sometimes the probation order predated the decision that a child was at risk, but more often, the case was already held as a child care case when the mother offended. The social worker would then recommend probation, ostensibly 'to give more focus' to existing work with the client, though it was evident the desire to 'protect' the mother and child from the effects of a fine or custodial sentence played a part. In any event, even after a probation order was made, we found no evidence in any of these cases that existing help or day to day management of the case was in any way altered by the order, which was generally ignored.

A number of probationers in this category were also the subject of additional requirements, which they blatantly disregarded. They were not breached because the social worker feared that a custodial sentence might result, and that this would be damaging to the child. In one case only, the mother was breached for non-compliance for failure to inform a change of address. Although this has happened some time earlier, the client was only breached, without warning, when it seemed that she and her family might move from the area entirely, making supervision of the children impossible.

> She really puts me off and I would never have another social worker...I couldn't trust them. I definitely couldn't trust them. And now when I talk to a social worker, I don't feel comfortable because I think they are going to be two-faced, be all nice and then do something behind your back.... I mean that was an awful shock I got when she had written that report, I never expected a thing of it. It came as a terrible shock.

Few probationers in this category wished to be interviewed. Of those who were, only two were at all positive about social work intervention, and even they had complaints. The general problem seemed to be that social worker and client goals were in conflict. At best, social work intervention was seen by the probationer to be irrelevant or misdirected; at worst, it was regarded as intrusive or devious.

Reactive. In these cases the probationer sets the pace and both contact and intervention are entirely on their terms. The social worker offers a friendly relationship and practical help and advice, but only as requested by the probationer. Work on the case is almost entirely reactive and any problems presented are dealt with as they occur. Actual supervision of the probationer is either almost or entirely absent. There is no structure for intervention, and no attempt to focus on the probationer's behaviour, offending or otherwise. The 'reactive welfare agent' is simply there to lend a sympathetic ear, and provide help and support when requested.

Social workers using this approach with probationers were usually strongly anti-authoritarian, viewing the judicial process with distaste, and custody with horror. They did everything they could to 'protect' their client from the court, ignoring non-compliance and not reporting further offences. In so far as they related to the court at all, it was as a buffer to prevent the client from coming into contact with it.

One might suppose probationers would be grateful for social work intervention so entirely geared to their needs and demands. Interestingly, those interviewed, while acknowledging that it was useful to have 'someone on your side', took their social workers' efforts very much for granted, and felt no corresponding obligation to change their ways:

Whenever I get into trouble, she's the first person I come to. Like when I got charged there a couple of months back with assault, I came to see her about it, and I've got to go back the third of next month. I'll come in and see her about that, I think she'll give me a...what's it called? A reference, she's my probation officer. I think she's writing one of them for me for when I go back up, saying that since I've been working and all that I've been a lot better. If I ever get into a fight or anything like that, I go down and tell her, she always takes a note of it. So if I was to get put up for it, I could turn round and say to them, 'wait, B's took a note of what I says, of what I've done, when it happened'. What my version is at the time when it happened, instead of about a month later when I get accused of it.

5.2.3 Minimal monitoring approach

What we describe as minimal monitoring does not belong clearly to either the 'court' or 'welfare' camps. Interactions between the social worker and probationer consist of brief, infrequent contacts, during which the social worker monitors the probationer in a cursory and superficial way, making no effective attempt to check progress. The absence of clear goals for the case, apart from a very general 'seeing how the probationer is doing', and the lack of any relationship distinguishes it very clearly from the 'supervising court agent' approach.

The monitoring approach might be identified with 'reporting' models of intervention described elsewhere (see e.g. Strathclyde Regional Council's development paper 1987) but the examples of 'minimal monitoring' which we encountered demonstrated much less well organised contact than recommended there, and could really hardly be termed 'an approach' at all. It may be that this type of supervision is simply the understandable reaction of hard-pressed workers to unresponsive probationers. Yet certainly, those on the receiving end were very clear and forthright in their view that it was 'a complete waste of time'. They were openly scornful of the superficial way they were supervised, feeling it had no impact on their lives, or on their offending.

She just comes in and says 'how are you doing? Are you all right?' That's it. I mean, I could be out doing loads of things...I could be breaking into houses and she wouldn't know any different. They just say 'Oh, right, fine come back in a fortnight'. I think they should maybe check up and see if you're telling the truth. What's the probation doing? Absolutely nothing, is it? It's like going to see your mate round the corner...It is just like calling in and having a chit-chat.

5.3 Relating intervention approaches

5.3.1 Intervention approach and social worker background

We considered it would be of interest to explore how far the identified intervention approaches related to the background and experience of social workers. Although this was somewhat complicated because some cases had several workers in the course of the order, and in others no work was done, we were able to establish a clear link in 62 of the cases where there had been social work intervention.

Not surprisingly, the 19 'specialists' - those with either previous specialist experience of offenders, or who were experienced generic workers with a special interest in probation - all used styles of supervision which were exclusively 'court agent' based, tending to adopt the befriending approach (10), rather than the rehabilitating (4) or supervising focus (5).

This contrasted with 'generic' workers, who had no special interest in probation, although some said they enjoyed the work. While many in this group (20 of the 43) also used court agent approaches, they tended, unlike the more specialist workers, to focus on rehabilitation (10) rather than befriending (only 1).

The greatest contrast however, was provided by the relatively inexperienced generic workers, with less than three years experience.. Three quarters of these adopted welfare agent styles of supervision. This finding came as no surprise, as the newly qualified workers interviewed tended to be very uncomfortable with the use of authority and uncertain about their role in relation to the court, supporting the findings of Fielding (1986) that newly qualified workers found more difficulty in 'collapsing the dichotomy' between care and control.

It is interesting that the small proportion of inexperienced workers who used the court agent approach, were either being supervised by seniors with a strong probation background, or had had supervision and practice of this kind during their training. Three unqualified social work assistants with the same approach also had many years practice experience and were interested in working with offenders. Conversely, interview data from both experienced and inexperienced workers using the welfare based approach, suggested that this style of work arises when workers are inadequately supervised, or are supervised by seniors whose main knowledge base and interests lie in other areas of work.

It must of course be stressed that the approaches outlined above are only tentative sketches of the practice we found. They are not based on any methodical sampling of social workers, but simply on the supervisors who were 'attached' to the selected probation cases, and whose representativeness is wholly unknown. The critical definitive element of the different approaches is the way the worker resolves the ambiguity between care and control, with this depending, at least in part, on the orientation of the worker to the court.

Nevertheless, as clarified earlier, the approaches are essentially styles of supervision, not types of social worker. In practice, while keeping within the same basic approach, some workers were well able to change the central focus. This was particularly so with experienced workers using the court agent approach, who seemed more able to modify their style of supervision according to the needs of the probationer.

Furthermore, it must also be noted that the adoption of a particular approach does not appear to be immutable. In view of the suggestion that the welfare agent approach was much more in evidence among inexperienced workers, and that most experienced workers used a court agent approach, it seems reasonable to induce that approach may change with experience. Indeed, between our initial and follow up interviews, two fairly inexperienced workers seemed to have changed their approach to supervision quite markedly, one as the result of an in-service training course, and the other through realisation of the problems inherent in the welfare agent approach.

Finally, we cannot begin to estimate the frequency with which the approaches described occur in practice, any more than we are able to say with any degree of assurance whether further research directed specifically at this issue might extend or modify our list of sketches.

5.3.2 Intervention approach and level of service

In the previous chapter, the level of service to probationers was examined and it is clear that there does seem to be some relation between this and the intervention approach adopted by social workers. In 70 cases we had sufficient information to cross classify the two variables. We found that 32 of the 42 social workers adopting court based approaches to supervision offered a 'good' (i.e. satisfactory and reasonable) level of service, and that in the 10 cases rated 'bad' (i.e. poor and very poor), the rating was due to non-allocation or poor recording.

In contrast, only six of the 18 workers using welfare based approaches were rated as giving a 'good' level of service, with the remaining twelve in the 'bad' category. To some extent this is tautological, as one of the characteristics of these approaches is the condoning of breaches, and this is simultaneously one definitive element of poor service. This of course also applies to the service consequences of minimal monitoring, where again only about a third (three out of ten) offered a 'good' level of service. Yet, nevertheless, the court based approach is clearly more likely to lead to 'good' service than is the welfare based approach.

5.3.3 Intervention approach and court area

We were able to cross classify intervention approaches and court area in 72 cases, of which 43 were court agent, 18 welfare agent based, with 11 cases receiving minimal monitoring only. The court agent approach to supervision was much more in evidence in the cases from the three small courts, with 61 per cent of probationers receiving this kind of intervention, compared to 40 per cent from the large court. Conversely, in supervision of cases from the large court, the welfare agent approach was more apparent, although the contrast was less marked, with 56 per cent of welfare based cases compared to 44 per cent which were court based. The majority of minimal monitoring cases also came from the large court (64 per cent) with the remainder distributed almost equally across the other three courts.

Looking more closely at the different social work districts serving the courts, the three with the highest proportion of court agent supervision all appeared to have significant features. In one district, for example, one social work office had an ex-compulsory care team, which was very 'probation oriented', and the other offices had a high proportion of experienced social workers, who said they enjoyed probation work, and were clearly able to use their authority and sanctions of the court as an integral part of their probation practice. There was also a lower rate of staff turnover than in the other offices covered by the research. Paradoxically, in this district, the tendency to use breach procedures more readily, largely explains the apparently low level of 'success' in outcome dealt with in the next chapter.

In the second district there was a special team servicing the court, in which high priority was given to probation. Here social workers were experienced and generally seemed comfortable, both in relation to court personnel and procedures, and in supervising probationers. In the third district, which was the only one of the three servicing the large court, there was a senior social worker in one office, who had a particular interest in probation and actively encouraged workers to attend court, and in another office there had previously been strong organisational links with area covered by the ex-compulsory care team.

In contrast, in the only district to show more use of welfare than court based supervision, the majority of cases were held by new or relatively inexperienced workers, several of whom admitted readily that they did not like 'court based' work and were ill at ease working within the structure and requirements of a probation order. As suggested earlier, adoption of welfare agent approaches may lead to inappropriate protection of and sometimes collusion with a client, through failure to breach for either non-compliance, or for the commission of a further offence. There is no doubt, from examination of individual cases, that some of the apparently 'successful' outcomes detailed in the next chapter, could be accounted for in this way.

5.3.4 Organisational aspects

Taking a more general view again, the organisation of social work service to the court, links between court and social work department, individual contact between social worker and court, and the degree to which sheriffs were satisfied with the service received, all varied considerably between the different districts covered by the research. The large court was serviced by a court based social work unit, headed by a senior social worker. The unit liaised with 15 area social work offices, as well as several sub-offices, which together covered the four city social work districts. One of the three smaller courts had a full time court social worker, a second had the services of a part time worker, and the third was serviced by one of the local social work teams with social workers attending court on a rota basis.

Although the above arrangements worked reasonably well, there were noticeable differences in the degree of direct personal contact social workers had with the courts. The various reasons for this have been given in earlier chapters. Sometimes it was a matter of policy, sometimes organisational factors had an effect, and sometimes the personal preferences of social workers and sheriffs came into play. Overall however, individual links were much more in evidence in the small courts, where they were seen by sheriffs as a valuable contribution to a responsive social work service.

While there were obvious advantages to having a court social worker, a special court team or a specialised unit within the court, one of the disadvantages we found was that other workers were not always able to build up court links, and neither did they attend court to speak to reports they had written. In this situation it was difficult for them, unless they were given the opportunity and encouragement, to acquire the confidence and expertise in working with the court, which helped to ensure an appropriate and satisfactory service to the probationer. As we saw in the previous chapter, the level of service to probationers tended to be higher in the smaller courts where workers also made more use of court agent approaches in supervision. As noted in Chapter 2, this was reflected in the greater satisfaction with social work service on the part of small court sheriffs.

5.4 Conclusion

5.4.1 Comparative acceptability

How acceptable are the different intervention approaches outlined, to those involved in the process and practice of probation. As we saw earlier, the sheriffs interviewed stressed the importance or regular and frequent contact, and made it clear that they expected significant breaches of the probation order to be reported promptly. On these grounds, the welfare based approaches to supervision, or minimal monitoring of an order, are unlikely to be acceptable to the courts.

However, sheriffs also identified as important the necessity for supervising social workers to use authority constructively; with an expectation that the probationer would be offered practical advice and guidance, support and encouragement, or counselling and specialist help, depending on the needs of the case. All these strands are found within the court based approaches, which are clearly closer to judicial definitions of good practice.

From the standpoint of social work management too, court based approaches to supervision seem more likely to be acceptable. The probation guidelines in use at the time of the research, laid stress on regular contact, the complementarity of care and control, and warned against condoning non-compliance. Again, on these counts neither welfare based approaches, nor minimal monitoring would be acceptable.

Last, but by no means least, from the probationer's point of view, maybe somewhat curiously at first glance, supervision based on the court agent approach was certainly more highly regarded and appreciated than either welfare based supervision, or mere minimal monitoring.

5.4.2 Ease of operation

From a purely practical standpoint, court agent approaches are inherently easier for social workers to manage effectively. Realistic and explicit recognition of the conditions and goals of the order fosters a shared perception of what probation is about and what is expected of the probationer and supervisor. Furthermore social workers are relieved of some of the worry many experience, by sharing the responsibility appropriately with the court.

In contrast, use of welfare agent approaches appears to lead to conflict and stress when deciding, for example, when to report a further offence, or whether to ignore non-compliance. Since social workers using these approaches feel they are working for the client rather than the court, notifying a breach is perceived as a personal act against the probationer. By failing to do so, on the other hand, the worker is protecting the probationer and able to carry on with 'welfare based' supervision. Sometimes of course, such a course of action is later discovered, when the loss of confidence of the court in that or other cases may be significant. All too frequently however, poor practice of this kind may unfortunately remain hidden in what is officially classified as 'successful completion of an order', more about which will be discussed in the next chapter.

6 Probation outcomes

6.1 Introduction

What constitutes a 'successful' probation order is much more difficult to define in theory than in practice. In chapter 2, for example, it was clear that sheriffs had no clear, single view. While a small minority defined success solely by the strictly legal criterion that no further offences had been committed during the course of the order, others thought that additional criteria also needed to be considered. These included less frequency in offending, signs of increased responsibility and maturity in the offender, and evidence that the probationer had been able to make positive use of the help available.

In chapter 5, we drew attention to the paradox that a 'successful' outcome - defined from the strictly formal and legalistic point of view - might well hide poor supervision, such as failure to breach for non-compliance. Conversely, a good standard of supervision and appropriate use of the sanctions available might end in a superficially 'unsuccessful' outcome.

Bearing these provisos in mind, we examined the outcomes for 84 probationers (two of the original 86 died during the course of their order). When assessed using the strictly legal criterion outlined above, 37 were successful, 37 were unsuccessful, and the remaining 10 were still continuing at the end of the research period. In the successful group, three orders were discharged early. In the unsuccessful group, 11 orders were continued and completed after breach, (using the broader criteria preferred by many sheriffs this outcome might well be regarded as successful) and 26 were terminated by the court, nine for non-compliance and 17 for commission of a further offence.

It would appear from the above figures that 37 orders had a totally satisfactory outcome in that they were completed without any further offences. However, if the process of these orders is examined more closely, a somewhat different picture emerges. In two cases, social workers failed to breach for regular and persistent non-compliance, and in another two cases further offences were not reported to the court. In yet another instance, where probation had been given for a social security offence, the social worker not only failed to inform the court of a further offence, but regularly colluded with the probationer over irregular earnings, on grounds of the probationer's financial hardship.

Similarly, in relation to the 10 continuing orders, two probationers had already committed further offences which had not been reported by the supervising social workers. It was again evident therefore, that, in some instances, what appeared to be a successful outcome, in fact concealed lack of appropriate action and poor practice by the supervisor.

Of the 11 cases which were completed after breach proceedings, nine were breached for further offences during the course of the order. While we have classified these strictly as unsuccessful, and they may well appear so at first glance, in practice they often indicated more active and appropriate intervention by the social worker, and a greater readiness to use the court in a constructive way as an integral part of the authority inherent in probation supervision. Certainly, as already stated, the majority of sheriffs did not necessarily regard such orders as failures.

It is perhaps not surprising that very few orders were continued after breach for non-compliance. Clearly the co-operation of the offender is essential to the probation process, and where this is not forthcoming there is little point in continuing the order. As one sheriff remarked:

> It strikes me that actual complying with the order is the most important part of it. I would see it as rather an odd situation if the supervisor was recommending that it continue, not withstanding the point that the probationer had failed to co-operate. I would be very reluctant to continue with the order in these circumstances.

The reluctance of some social workers to breach on grounds of non-compliance, was discussed in chapters 4 and 5. Overall nine of the 84 orders ended with a breach of this kind. Of the 17 which were breached for further offence, five were actually breached on dual grounds. It is perhaps significant that, even though non-compliance had been a consistent feature of these cases, breach proceedings were only instituted once a further offence had been committed.

The very small number of early discharges is understandable given the comments of social workers presented in chapter 4. The mechanisms of applying to the court, the time involved, and the fact that the recommendation might not be accepted, were all factors which discouraged supervisors from exercising this option. Only in very few cases did social workers use it as a reward for achievement or as a boost to both probationer and social worker.

Before moving on to look in more detail at some potentially researchable relationships between background variables and outcome 'success', it is worth considering briefly the rates of 'success' in the court areas studied. Overall, of the 74 completed cases, 39 were from the three small courts and 35 from the one large court. Legalistically defined 'success' and 'failure' was fairly evenly distributed, with 20 successes in the three small courts and 17 in the large one.

This picture is easily understandable in two of the small courts, with a high proportion of first and early offenders and, as one might expect, a high proportion of successful outcomes (15 of 26, or 58 per cent). However, two of the social work districts serving the large court had an extremely high proportion of young persistent and adult offenders, yet also showed a reasonably high proportion of successful outcomes (10 of 19, or 53 per cent). Moreover the third small court and one of the two remaining social work districts serving the large court, each with a similar distribution of offender types, nevertheless showed different levels of successful orders (5 of 13, or 38 per cent and 4 of 7, or 57 per cent respectively). Finally, the remaining district serving the large court, with an equal division between first and early offenders, and young persistent and adult offenders, appeared to have the lowest success rate of all (3 of 9, or 33 per cent). In order to try and make sense of these outcomes we need to consider them in more detail.

6.2 Outcome and intervention approach

It was possible to match an intervention approach with a case outcome in 61 cases. In general, court based approaches did marginally better than welfare ones or minimal monitoring. Of the 37 cases where a court based approach was adopted, 23 (62 per cent) were successful. Of the 24 cases where a welfare approach or minimal monitoring was used, only 13 (54 per cent) had a successful outcome.

For low tariff offenders, the proportion of successful:unsuccessful outcomes was high (23:7, or 77 per cent), and those supervised from a court based perspective had a higher success rate than the remainder (16:4, or 80 per cent; and 7:4, or 64 per cent, respectively). Within this category the proportion of successful to unsuccessful outcomes for first offenders, remained high irrespective of the intervention approach adopted (18:4, or 82 per cent), although two of the 'successful' outcomes in the welfare based group are deceptive as one had an unreported further offence and the other had not been reported for non-compliance. For early offenders the numbers are very small indeed and the success rate reasonable (5:3, or 63 per cent). They, too, seemed to do well whatever the intervention approach.

For high tariff offenders overall, success was less frequent than failure (13:18, or 42 per cent), whether a court based approach was adopted (7:10, or 41 per cent) or a welfare or monitoring one (6:8, or 43 per cent). However, outcomes for young persistent offenders were reasonably balanced (6:7, or 46 per cent) whatever the intervention approach adopted. Adult recidivists showed the worst success:failure rate at 7:11 (39 per cent), with the proportion of failures receiving court based supervision higher (4:7, or 36 per cent) than in the other group (3:4, or 43 per cent). However, one of the 'successes' in the latter group again conceals an unreported further offence. It is also worth noting that, if we take the broader view of 'success' discussed earlier, rather than the strictly legalistic viewpoint, the adult recidivist picture changes somewhat. Using these wider criteria, four of the seven 'court based supervision' failures went on to complete their probation after being breached, as did two of the 'welfare based' group. In each of these instances the worker 'held on' to the probationer, with appropriate backing from the court, and felt, at the end, that the order had been a success, as did the probationer concerned.

While the numbers involved are so small and the trends so slight, that any perceived relationship may well be due to chance, the overall pattern is borne out by an examination of the process of individual cases. This suggests that social worker approach interacts with the probationer response to influence the success of the outcome. The interaction is a dynamic one, in which the social worker may adapt his intervention approach to fit in with what the probationer will allow him to do. On the other hand, the probationer's motivation may change as a result of a particular intervention approach, sometimes with surprising results. A few examples of typical interactions will make the point.

Probationers who seem to show the 'Cry for Help' response, typical of first offenders, have identifiable problems to work on, often of a practical nature, and are often clearly in a state of crisis when the order is made. This gives social workers something definite they can respond to immediately and sympathetically. Such probationers are likely to be co-operative anyway, because of their high commitment, but this is enhanced as the order progresses by the fact that their perceived needs are clearly met, and because they can foresee a positive outcome. They attend regularly and work hard on identified problems. Authority is not a major element in intervention, since most offenders of this kind comply with the order and do not re-offend. They therefore do well whatever the orientation of the social worker.

Case A. Case A was a married women, aged 26, on probation for a first shoplifting offence, arising from serious financial and marital problems. She received help from a recently qualified social worker, whose approach was clearly that of a pro-active carer. Authority did not form part of the contact, but the probationer was very co-operative. Although the social worker was keen to work on mutual goals, and indeed drew up regular written contracts with the probationer, it was clear in interview that the probationer's perceptions and expectations in fact conflicted with those of the social worker, and that she was dissatisfied with some aspects of the service. Nevertheless she was very grateful for the help she did receive, used it well, made some progress and did not re-offend.

Probationers who are at a turning point, such as some adult recidivists, also often have identifiable problems, which they recognise and welcome help with. However, in general, the problems are not simply external ones of a practical nature which can be 'fixed' for the probationer by the social worker. They are much more likely to be long standing, embedded in the probationer's own life style, and requiring personal change by the probationer himself. The supervisor is therefore required to adopt an approach which will actively encourage the probationer to effect changes in his behaviour. Social work intervention in such cases needs to lay more stress on authority, confrontation, and what probationers themselves generally referred to as 'pushing'.

Social workers often found these probationers rewarding in the long term, but they were clearly very hard work. Changes take time and effort; there are lapses and re-offences to deal with, all of which create additional work for the supervisor, and demand continual help and support for the probationer. These probationers need a high degree of commitment, focus and forcefulness from their social workers, which we found particularly in the rehabilitative focus of the court based approach, as in the following case:

Case B. Case B was an intelligent young adult recidivist, with a long history of offences, all arising from alcohol abuse. He received help from a social worker adopting a court based, rehabilitative approach to supervision. While keen to make the most of his 'last chance', the probationer was initially rather casual about regular contact and work on his problem, missing appointments and maintaining that he could cope with a 'controlled drinking' programme. The social worker took a firm line over attendance, and used a further offence very constructively to ram home her message about the effect alcohol was having on the probationer's life. With his consent she enrolled the help of his cohabitee to monitor his drinking and pushed him into Further Education courses to improve his prospects for the future. In the second half of his order the probationer made good progress, opting for an alcohol-free regime, enrolling in computer classes, and not reoffending. In interviews with the researcher he was extremely positive about the effect probation had had on his life.

If a purely welfare based approach is adopted with probationers like this, the client is likely to use the social worker simply as a prop, a source of unending sympathy and help in periodically picking up the pieces, without any change taking place, as in this case, which drifted along without any clear focus or sense of direction:

Case C. Case C was a middle aged lady with a long history of offences, all arising from alcohol abuse, for which she had received long term intensive psychiatric treatment, as well as social work help and support. She had had two previous periods of probation. Supervised on this occasion by a social worker experienced in child care, but new to probation, the approach to supervision was entirely welfare based. Although the social worker was conscientious, she saw her role only as offering general social work support. At the time the order was granted, the probationer was already receiving a lot of informal help and support from a previous social worker who had become a personal friend, and because of this, she had asked for the order to be made out to another social worker. Despite this, the new supervisor was drawn into a friendship role with the probationer, in which authority played no part. The probationer was given a high level of service, with a great deal of emotional and practical support, for which she was very grateful. However, she re-offended three times during the order. In interview the social worker described her role in relation to these offences as providing encouragement and reassurance to the probationer and mediating with the court in an attempt to prevent a custodial disposal. On the first two occasions she recommended that probation continue. However, after a third re-offence which also involved a suicide attempt, the probationer turned against the social worker, complaining of inadequate service. The social worker finally reluctantly recommended that the order be terminated, and the probationer received a six month custodial sentence.

Probationers who regard probation as irrelevant (such as many young persistent offenders and some adult recidivisits) do not recognise themselves as having any real problems with which they want help. Thus the social worker has little focus to work with, as attempts to get the probationer to tackle problems identified by the social worker are likely to be resisted. Faced with this situation, social workers often seemed driven into adopting a variety of approaches. Sometimes this consisted merely of minimal monitoring, reduced to almost a social level, although sometimes accompanied by warnings about associates and penalties for re-offending. Since the probationer's aim in these situations is usually to avoid any hassle, they may very well comply superficially with the order, by attending more or less regularly (or as much as they need to do to avoid being breached) and taking care not to be caught offending during the period of the order. Little change takes place however, and they may continue to offend and ultimately be caught, as in this case:

Case D. Case D was a 20 year old persistent offender, on probation for theft. After an initial interview with an intake senior during which he was advised of the conditions of the order, the probationer was given three appointments, all of which he kept, during his one year order. On each occasion he was seen by a different social worker, each of whom made brief enquiries as to how he was getting on, and asked him to get in touch if there were any problems. When last seen, several months before the order ended, the third social worker (newly qualified) recorded that the probationer did not need to be seen again, as there were no problems, and he was unlikely to re-offend. The order was completed 'successfully'. However, when contacted for interview by a researcher only two months after completion of the order, the probationer's father informed us that his son was on the point of emerging from a custodial sentence for a further offence, committed during the course of the order.

Sometimes, a reactive welfare approach may well be welcomed by probationers like this, who accept or request help from the social worker, of a kind they perceive as useful, such as obtaining help from the DHSS, or acting as an ally against the judicial system. The probationer effectively uses social work intervention to meet his own ends, and if these are illegal, the social worker may be drawn into collusion, and to committing irregularities himself. The social worker has the impression that he is offering a service, but in fact the probationer's offending pattern is untouched. Consider this case:

Case E. Case E was a 25 year old adult recidivist with a long history of convictions, on his first period of probation, and supervised by a recently qualified worker, adopting a welfare based approach to supervision. The probationer received a reasonable level of service and was co-operative about keeping appointments. Social work help focused on responding to the probationer's needs for emotional support over the break-up of his marriage, and on helping him find employment. The order was completed 'successfully'. However, when the probationer was interviewed shortly before it ended, he disclosed to the researcher that he had in fact been convicted and fined for a further offence during the course of the order. The social worker had not reported this as he thought the probationer had not been charged. The probationer was unemployed when seen, but 'making a bit on the side' through occasional painting and decorating jobs while drawing benefit. The social worker's view was that such illegality 'is between him and the DHSS', and in the interviewer's presence was arranging for him to take on more paid work of this kind - for the Social Work Department!

85

Alternatively, the social worker may adopt the court based rehabilitative approach in order to try to push the probationer into recognising he has a problem, and then into working on it, perhaps using court proceedings over a further offence to drive the lesson home. How successful this is probably depends on whether or not the probationer's situation and motivation are ripe for change. If they are not, the social worker's efforts are likely to be seen as interfering, and strongly resented, and the probationer will turn against her with the 'intrusive' type of response noted earlier. If, however, the probationer is ready for change, this method may be very successful. The only two probationers who started off seeing probation as 'irrelevant' and ended up highly motivated were won over as a result of a court based rehabilitation approach to supervision. Here is one of them:

Case F. Case F was a young persistent offender, with a history of offences linked to alcohol abuse. He admitted he was initially pleased to get probation, as he considered it an easy option, and thought he would be able to go along with it, without it really interfering with his pattern of criminal behaviour. However his social worker, who was very experienced, took a much firmer and more confrontational line that he expected, coupled with real and clearly manifested concern for his future. While the probationer initially resented her 'interference' he gradually began to recognise the need to tackle his drinking problem. Matters were brought to a head when she breached him on grounds of a further offence, with a recommendation that probation should be continued, because of the efforts he was making and the improvement in his attitude. Thereafter, he developed a good relationship with the worker and, within a clear authority structure, co-operated well and made excellent progress. Unfortunately his social worker left the department, and the case was transferred to a supervisor who adopted a very minimal monitoring approach, only seeing the probationer at his request if needed; thereafter contact was irregular and infrequent. During the final months of the order, a personal crisis arose, but the probationer felt unable to seek help from a worker whom he hardly knew, and who he felt had shown very little interest in him. He began drinking again, and when interviewed by the researcher after the end of the order, had recently re-offended.

As can be seen from an in depth analysis of cases, the picture provided by outcome statistics alone is somewhat misleading in measuring the proportion of 'successful' orders. This is due first to the complexity of defining what actually constitutes success, so that we were obliged to accept a strictly legal, formal and minimum standard. Second, having decided on a definition of success, this itself may actually measure poor practice by the supervisor, rather than sustained effort by the probationer.

Nevertheless, though the numbers are small and the differences slight, it seemed to us, taking account of all the data available, that variations in social work approach had little impact on outcome for first and early offenders. For young persistent offenders and adult recidivists, the court based approaches to supervision, particularly if focused on 'rehabilitation' could be particularly useful. Conversely, welfare based approaches appeared unhelpful to these groups.

So far in this chapter, we have considered the relationship between the outcome of probation and the intervention approach, which, in chapter 5, we have already linked to the background and experience of the social worker. There are of course other factors which may influence variations in outcome, one of which is the level of service probationers receive (see chapter 4).

6.3 Outcome and level of service

It was possible to match level of service with case outcome for 72 cases. It is immediately striking that level of service alone does not necessarily generate successful outcomes. Those probationers who had a 'good' service had a succcess:fail ratio of 22:19 (a 54 per cent success rate), while those receiving a 'poor' service were only a little less well served, with a ratio of 15:16 (a 48 per cent success rate).

How does the picture change if we if we introduce the further variable of offender tariff? Overall the 'success' rate for low tariff offenders was high (23:8, or 74 per cent), and for high tariff offenders low (14:27, or 34 per cent). When both groups had good service, low tariff offenders still 'succeeded' much more frequently (16:4, or 80 per cent) than high tariff ones (6:15, or 29 per cent). When both groups had 'bad' service, low tariff offenders still 'succeeded' reasonably often (7:4, or 64 per cent) with high tariff ones apparently doing better at 8:12 (or 40 per cent) than they did with good service. We see that first and early offenders did well regardless of level of service or style of intervention. However, what of the rather curious result that high tariff offenders appeared to do better with a poorer level of service?

Again, we need to get behind the figures to see what is actually going on. Looking at particular cases which had a 'bad' service, but 'successful' outcome, it becomes clear that a number of these concealed unreported further offences or non-compliance. The extent of this however, varied between different offender groups. For example, the successful outcomes of the four first offenders who had poor service all appeared genuine, with no unreported further offences or non-compliance. In the case of the three early offenders, two had unreported further offences. In the young persistent offender group, one of the poor service 'successes' had unreported non-compliance, and one of the three 'successful' adult recidivists had an unreported further offence.

6.4 Outcome and length of order

In 74 cases we were able to match length of order with case outcome. In general the success rate was higher for probationers on short orders of one year or 18 months (31:23, or 57 per cent), than for those with longer orders of two or three years (6:14, or 30 per cent). Within this, however, high tariff offenders succeeded far more frequently on the shorter orders than the longer ones (13:17, or 43 per cent; and 1:12, or 8 per cent respectively).

If and how far tariff rating explains the higher success rate of shorter orders is open to question. Once again, we have reached the limit of analytic ability given the data we have. All we are able to say is that we have found no evidence that shorter periods of probation are less effective than longer orders, and what trends we have detected suggest that they may in fact be more so. There are, however, two ways of explaining this:

First, from the social work point of view, it may be that a shorter order more easily concentrates the efforts of supervisor and probationer on achieving progress on identified problems and goals. This explanation is in line with research on the effectiveness of task-centred work, which suggests that time-limited purposeful contact is more effective than open ended, less focused activity. A number of the experienced social workers interviewed were of the opinion that the most useful work with probationers is usually done in the first few months of the order. This coincided with our own experience of interviewing probationers at different points during the order. Although there were of course exceptions, most of those we saw on several occasions, showed most change early in the probation period.

Second, a more cynical perspective suggests that the shorter the order, the less chance there is of the probationer becoming engaged in nefarious activities, or of being caught doing so. A shorter order is thus a less stringent test of the probationer's reformation, and he may 'pass' more easily than on a longer order. This reasoning ties in with the view expressed by one sheriff, that one purpose of probation is for the probationer to prove himself of good behaviour, and this cannot be done adequately if the order is too short, or is terminated before its due date. This view however, is not borne out by analysis of the process of our cases. If longer orders produce worse outcomes by allowing offending behaviour to re-emerge gradually, one would expect the re-offences to occur in the later stages of longer orders. In fact the reverse was true: most longer orders ending in breach on these grounds, were breached during the first few months of the order, especially in the adult recidivist group.

6.5 Outcome and probationer gender

Probationer gender could be matched with case outcome in 76 cases. Overall, female offenders succeeded more often than they failed (16:7, or a 70 per cent success rate); and the reverse was true for male offenders (21:30, or 41 per cent success rate). Looking at offender types more closely however, females were over represented in the first offender category, with its generally high success rate, but very much under represented in the other three groups.

When outcome is broken down into offender groups therefore, the difference between gender outcomes largely disappears for first and early offenders. For low tariff offenders the female success:failure ratio was 13:4 (76 per cent) compared with a male success ratio of 10:4 (71 per cent). In the case of high tariff offenders there is a greater difference, with female probationers having a success ratio of 3:3 (50 per cent) and males a success ratio of 11:26 (30 per cent).

6.6 Conclusion

As indicated earlier, given the general lack of consensus about the specific aims and objectives of probation and what constitutes a successful order, outcome is a complex and complicated concept to measure. In addition, what appears to a successful outcome using a strictly limited legal definition, may conceal failure to comply on the part of the probationer and, or the commission of further unreported offences. Even taking account of these difficulties and limitations however, several tentative conclusions do begin to emerge in relation to the variables considered.

First, low tariff offenders, particularly first offenders, have a much better outcome in completion terms than do young persistent offenders or adult recidivists.

Second, differences in level of service to probationers, do not seem to affect outcome to any great extent, except for 'very poor' service which shows a markedly worse outcome than the other three groups. There is a slight indication that service level may be more important to adult recidivists, who may be particularly vulnerable to very poor levels of service.

Third, first and early offenders tend to do well irrespective of the intervention approach used by social workers. There does however, seem to be some discernible relationship pattern between the intervention approach to supervision and the outcome of the order, with young persistent offenders and adult recidivists. In these groups, positive outcomes are more likely to occur when a court agent approach is adopted with probationers, particularly if it has a 'rehabilitative' focus. Court based approaches to supervision appear to be used mainly by experienced workers, with either a background of work with offenders, or a particular interest in this area of work, backed up by encouragement and good supervision from senior staff.

Fourth, two variables which we initially thought might be influential on outcome are probationer gender and length of order. Later analysis has confirmed the view that probationer gender does not seem significantly influential once offender type has been taken into account. Length of order, on the other hand, does appear to show some association with outcome, suggesting that shorter orders are certainly no less effective than longer ones, and may indeed be more so.

Finally, the way the numerous variables combine and interact have an important and influential effect on the process and practice of probation, leading to differential outcomes at individual, team and area level. We have merely identified, and tentatively suggested, the possible significance of certain of these variables and the relationships between them. What is now required is further development of the ideas and research questions suggested by our findings, and rigorous and systematic testing of the hypotheses which have emerged.

7 Conclusion

7.1 Probationers and social workers

7.1.1 Probationers on the appropriateness of probation

Only a few probationers expressed any views in terms of the most suitable type of offender or offence for probation. Not surprisingly, those who did tended to cite the offender and offence types which mirrored their own situation. Types of offender for whom probation was felt to be particularly suitable were first and early offenders, not yet caught up in a criminal network; and long term offenders who had not had probation before, and who had been in and out of jail:

> For some people who have never had a chance of probation it could maybe help them. People who have always had 3 months, 60 days, 6 months, 18 months, 2 years - never ever got the chance of probation. I suppose it could maybe help them, because they might say, 'well they gave me a chance. I've got to show, you know, that I am worthy of it.' You maybe just get one in ten that would buck his ideas up and, you know, do it.

The same probationer was insistent that only once chance should be allowed. He continued:

> Providing they've not had it before, right enough. If they have had probation before and they've just abused it, then obviously they would just abuse it again, unless circumstances have changed. I mean, if they were abusing it say when they were nineteen, twenty, running about with boys, and they are maybe twenty seven or twenty eight now, and they are maybe married with a couple of children, I think they should get the

chance because things are different for them. I mean they know they've got to try.

Although most of the probationers who expressed a view focused on the suitability of the offender rather than the offence, the seriousness of the offence was also mentioned. Minor offences were seen as most suitable - defined by one probationer in the following way:

> Minor offences. Car thefts, now that can vary. You can have a car theft which is involved with an accident, or you could have the odd car thief who just steals a car and takes it from A to B and leaves it. For the ones who are stealing the car to wreck it, then they should get a (prison) sentence. The ones who use it just to get from A to B, then I think that should be the sort for probation.

Others stressed the welfare component, seeing probation as a response to the need for help, often with family problems. There was agreement however, that the motivation of the offender was of crucial importance, based on a genuine desire to keep out of trouble and make a go of things.

> I think that for probation to be of any use whatsoever you have to have someone who is willing to get help. It would be no use for somebody who was forced into it. The motivation has to come from you, no question about it.

7.1.2 Probationers on factors assisting success

Over half the probationers interviewed expressed an opinion about this, showing considerable agreement about the two most important factors. The first, already mentioned in the previous section, was the crucial importance of the attitude and motivation of the probationer. As we have seen earlier, some started off with the view that probation was either irrelevant to their needs, or that it was merely a framework within which they could continue with their usual offending behaviour pattern without too much disruption to their lives. In these instances, the chances of real success were slight.

Second, probationers were clear about what was required of the supervisor, good supervision being the other most important factor in the probation process. Genuine interest, appropriate availability, the willingness to develop a good relationship with the probationer, and the ability to handle authority clearly and comfortably, encouraging and 'pushing' the probationer when necessary. Given probationers' perceptions of the importance of the supervisor's role, how satisfied were they with the supervision they received?

7.1.3 Probationers on the quality of social work.

Of the 43 probationers interviewed, 42 were assessed by two researchers, making independent ratings, on their general satisfaction with the quality of social work received.

The majority (30) were very, reasonably, or mildly satisfied (18, 2 and 10 respectively). One was neutral, and of the remaining 11, most (7) were only mildly dissatisfied. However, while not wishing to undervalue the excellent service which some probationers had received, it does seem as if a few were uncritical either because of low expectations, or because of loyalty to their social worker.

For instance one probationer was only seen twice during the first seven months of the order by his first social worker (he was subsequently transferred and seen regularly by a second) yet he strongly resisted the suggestion that the social worker had been less than helpful. Indeed he claimed:

> Well at that stage I think it would be unfair to him to say anything other than the fact that he knew I was there (at the residential hostel) and ostensibly they were set up to help me. Because he wasn't going to interfere along those lines, it would be very very unfair to him to say that he didn't offer to help.

All probationers were asked directly whether they could think of any improvements which could be made, but only a few could. Understandably those with least experience of offending and the judicial system had least to say, and most suggestions came from those with a long history of involvement with the courts. Perhaps surprisingly, the most frequent mentioned suggestion was that probation should be 'stricter', with closer monitoring. Several probationers agreed that it was too easy to 'con' social workers into believing they were behaving well.

Several probationers pointed out that monitoring on Community Service Orders was much stricter than on probation, and one probationer favoured a return to 'separate' probation officers for the same reason. Another suggestion was that probation should be more activity based, both by undertaking voluntary work during the day, and some sort of club type provision for the evenings:

> You feel funny just letting your friends go into the pub and you just running up the road. It would be better if there was a scheme that you could go to every night or something, a club... as part of the probation. During the day too, when you are unemployed, probation should give you something to do. There should be some facilities or something instead of just sitting in the house if you are unemployed, or walking the streets.... That's why you get into trouble. Activities would help you keep out of

trouble, or fighting or drinking or whatever. If you drink, you fight. There should be like a restart, an office up there too, just to sit and write letters to firms, and phone firms out of the yellow pages.

Two probationers pointed to the need for probation hostels:

See the likes of that hostel thing, it would be like a family. Maybe just say ten in the hostel, a tele-room and all that..(Q. And have someone there?) Say a man and a woman. They would be staff, but they wouldn't be staff to you because you are an adult now. They'd just be your kind of mates, know what I mean? Do a check that the meals get made, the doors get locked or something. Just all take turns in cooking the meals or something. And to hold meetings, you know, open meetings where everybody talks about things.

7.1.4 Social workers on alternatives in supervision

None of the probationers in our sample had systematically received any other kind of intervention from their supervisors than traditional one to one casework. While this was appropriate for many probationers, social workers nevertheless, also drew attention to the need for more group work, the setting up of probation clinics and the development of self help groups. In several offices covered by the research, there had apparently been abortive attempts to introduce more 'creative' forms of supervision, but we were told that efforts were hampered by insufficient time, and lack of opportunity and encouragement to develop such initiatives.

As a possible solution to many of these identified difficulties, many social workers favoured the idea of specialist probation workers within generic teams. Several pointed out that allowing workers to specialise was likely to improve the quality of service to the courts and to probationers because:

There's a strong parallel between people's preferences and people's abilities. If they have a preference in a particular area of work, generally they have good ability in that area too.

One experienced generically trained worker, with a special interest in work with offenders nicely summed up the general view:

I'm aware of the fact that probation is not being used as much by the courts now as it once was. I suspect a lot of that is to do with the local authorities' low priority for probation. It's to do with this fact of lost confidence, to some degree, in some of the workers. Some of them, unfortunately being generic, have not got a great deal of experience, and to some extent are intimidated by offenders. And consequently that leads to poor service for the offender, because the worker is unable to use himself appropriately for the benefit of the client.

He concluded:

> I believe that the specialist thing has to be developed a bit further. It has to be seen to be effective, in order to gain the confidence of the court again, in order to provide an adequate service for the clientele.

7.2 Sheriffs' views

7.2.1 On better liaison with social work departments

Most sheriffs did not want a return to the past, with a separate probation service. Even the few who nostalgically felt the past was preferable, thought the cost of returning to it would be too high. One commented sadly:

> I think it would probably be better with a separate service, but that does not mean that I want more upheavals. I think they haven't enough people or time to do it.

Many could see room for improvement in the current system however. One explained his ideas of how it could be further developed, an important element being the development of the role of the court liaison officer:

> They've been around for a long time, but I think that if anything they have improved, rather than the reverse, over the last few years.

Effective and efficient communication at this level is seen as the basis of good liaison between court and social work, especially when, for various reasons, individual links are difficult to make and maintain. Neither are such links always wanted. One sheriff said that he 'didn't like having meetings with social workers who are directly involved in a case', and another agreed:

> One doesn't want to have a conversation about things that the accused person doesn't know about, something that is hidden. One has to watch that sort of thing.

7.2.2 On using probation more frequently

Given the broad desire for more non-custodial sentences, what would persuade sheriffs to use probation more often as a disposal? Although some of those who felt that probation was limited to certain offender types thought they were already using it as much as possible, most agreed that there were two factors which would encourage more use of probation as a disposal. The first of these was more probation recommendations from social workers. One sheriff told us:

> I probably use it sparingly, primarily because the number of recommendations for probation isn't very great, and I won't put somebody on probation unless there is a recommendation for it in the report.

Another added:

> I very often put someone on probation if I'm asked to do so, and I think I'd put more people on probation if it was recommended more often. I am a little disappointed about the frequency of recommendations. I have seen cases where I thought probation would have had some part, and it has not been recommended.

The second factor mentioned frequently was the need for more knowledge of and confidence in probation supervision. One sheriff said, that from some of the examples which had come before him in court, he felt there was a need for some 'general tightening up'. Another was more specific:

> Some of us feel that if we were assured that supervision was to be adequate, that there would be no delays in allocation and so forth, and that in cases that required it there would be strict supervision - because supervision is bound to vary from individual to individual - if we were assured of all these things we might be disposed to use it more often.

A number of sheriffs confessed that they didn't feel social workers were as 'down to earth' as the old probation officers, with two stating categorically that they would use probation more if workers were more like 'hard headed probation officers':

> 'Harder headed probation officers' covers it all. It covers the whole range of activities, and there is nothing would encourage me to use probation more than having a practical hard headed probation officer.

The need for probation hostels, to provide a firmer framework for supervision, was also mentioned, particularly for the young, for whom the alternative is often:

> A case of imprisonment, simply to give him a roof over his head and a bit if discipline. The roof over his head part could be dealt with by a hostel, and the probation itself gives that wee bit of discipline.

Another expanded:

> There are definitely cases, particularly with youngsters 16 or 17 age level, where a probation hostel would be very valuable. The kind of boy who has got into trouble and the instant reaction of the parents is to throw him

96

out of the house. Where left to their own devices they are likely to get into further trouble, but a controlled environment like a probation hostel might very well be an improvement. The availability of probation hostels would open up a number of cases which might well be appropriate for probation.

7.2.3 On improvements to probation supervision

Besides being asked what specific factors would encourage them to use probation more, sheriffs were also asked to suggest ways in which they thought the probation service to the courts and to offenders could be improved. Again the need for more formalised communication between the court and social work departments was given high priority, as well as the need for more general information about what actually happens when someone is placed on probation.

As indicated in chapter 2, the majority of sheriffs had little idea of what service probationers received, and while a small minority felt this was not their concern, most were keen to know more. One way of filling this knowledge gap and providing more consistent feedback might be the introduction of completion reports at the end of an order as is done with community service orders. The majority of sheriffs welcomed this idea and saw a number of potential benefits:

> If a completion report was going to be made in all cases, that should increase the degree of supervision. So they can say at the end of the period 'he was seen on so many occasions and he was given this, that and the other advice and support'.

and:

> Such a system would lead to an improvement in mutual understanding and confidence, in the actual operation of probation, and in what the standards of the operation of probation are.

It was also mentioned that the systematic provision of completion reports could influence sentencing practice:

> It is certainly a very good idea because it would give us some indication of how successful probation actually is in terms of working for particular people. Apart from anything else, you get people coming up when they have been on probation, and unless you call for another report, you don't know how the previous period of probation has gone. There are, if you like, regulars, and if you were getting reports at the end of the period, that would be very useful.

One or two sheriffs however, were of the opinion that it was impossible to generalise from feedback of this nature about a particular probationer. As one said:

> If you get a report that it has turned out very nicely, apart from gratifying one's ego, I don't see the point. I don't remember these things, especially if it's a year or two after it's happened.

and another added:

> Supposing they give a completion report and it has been successful in their view. So what? Am I to say that because I get reports that on the average case it has been unsuccessful, I shouldn't put another person on probation?

Several sheriffs told us that occasionally, but very infrequently, they had asked for a progress report during the course of an order. This was only done in very special circumstances, such as in the following case of a mother who had ill treated a child:

> I spoke to the social worker at the time of making the order, and I said 'do you think this would help?' And she said 'yes, I think it probably would'. She brought the child with her and the social worker showed that an immense amount of work had been done already. So we had a nice chat and the child pinched my ruler and got away with it! But that was an example of bringing the person back to impress upon them that this wasn't just another thing that they had managed to shove aside.

In general however, there was no support for mandatory progress reports, on the grounds that social workers should be left to supervise probationers without the interference of the court. As sheriffs pointed out, existing breach procedures are there if the probationer 'doesn't perform well' and 'if they are working all right, there is really no need for the court to be further involved'. There was also the question of court powers in relation to progress reports:

> There would have to be some complementary powers to go with it. However, the idea that every order was going to be reviewed at the halfway stage, and the court had powers to act, would be extremely salutary.

It was also felt that progress reports, as a matter of course, would cause considerable practical difficulties for courts and social work departments already struggling to keep on top of ever increasing work loads. One sheriff remarked that he had occasionally asked for an interim report six months into an order, but had now given this up, having been told that it created extra work and administrative difficulties for everyone concerned. Another seconded this view:

> Ideally, I think I would like reports every three months or so, but manpower problems mean that is not possible. They would be too busy writing me reports to supervise properly.

Yet another idea put forward to improve probation was that sheriffs might be more involved in the training of social workers. This would be of mutual benefit, in that sheriffs would become more aware of the social work process, and social workers would more readily understand some of the difficulties and dilemmas faced by sheriffs.

There was also a strong body of opinion in favour of more specialisation by social workers, but within a generic social work service. One area particularly, which sheriffs thought would benefit from greater specialisation, was the preparation of social enquiry reports. One very experienced sheriff summed up a widespread view:

> The views expressed by some social workers are nothing less than ridiculous, and I have heard a similar opinion to mine expressed from the Court of Appeal. I would dearly love to get a good realistic report. The reports we get are generally not realistic and not helpful.

The generic structure of social work departments was seen as having distinct advantages however:

> The beauty of the generic service is that the social worker nowadays has more chance to go into other avenues than the old probation officers had.

One even likened the structural role of the probation supervisor to that of the family doctor:

> I can see the advantage of the generic structure. Social workers have a very wide remit, and a very wide knowledge of child abuse, housing policy and so on. There are often so many aspects to a probationer's case. I would assume that one of the things a social work probation officer would do, is to be able to be like a general practitioner in medicine, who would have accessible to him or her, specialised services.

7.2.4 On other additions to current service

One possibility which a number of sheriffs said they would like to see was the availability of community service as a condition of probation. In fact this was already available to some of the sheriffs interviewed, depending on the arrangements in the different social work areas. Some had community service schemes, some didn't; some schemes were linked to probation, some weren't. In any event sheriffs differed in the exact arrangements they would like to see.

Of the 15 who commented on this issue, two thirds saw community service as a direct alternative to custody and quite different from probation. They saw no advantage in any formal linking of the two, and indeed, several thought it would lead to confusion and lack of clarity in sentencing. The general view in this group was that, if a probationer needed help, it was perfectly possible to make a probation order as well as giving community service.

The remainder wanted to have a linked as well as a separate option, feeling there were occasions, when sentencing, which required 'care and control as well as positive development in the form of work'.

Greater use of additional requirements was another area of possible development where sheriffs had mixed feelings. While a requirement to attend a particular centre, for example, was felt to add structure and discipline in theory, sheriffs were less sure about the effect in practice. In fact there was a feeling that social workers had a tendency to 'wash their hands' of a case, once it had been 'taken over' by a specialist agency. Several referred to cases where they felt this had happened, or where they had no idea what kind of contact had been maintained between the social worker and the probationer:

> I could understand that, because basically the problem was that the person had a history of 'illness' if you like, and really it was for the doctors to decide how he should be treated and so on. But I don't think the social worker should just lose track, because there are bound to be areas where the social worker can supplement what the doctor is doing. I mean the person is not attending the clinic every day.

and another example:

> The offender has told me he hasn't been on drugs for six months, and I have no reason to suspect otherwise. It is probably quite true, but whether they have actually investigated you never know. If someone is attending an alcohol centre, whether they just report to the social worker now and again and say 'well, I've been this week' and they say 'that's fine'...well, you never know whether they actually check up on it.

Besides some concern that social workers were too readily 'accepting the probationer's word for it' in such situations, there was also doubt about the value of compelling a person to receive treatment, unless he was motivated to do so. Realistically however, it was recognised that a specific requirement was sometimes necessary in order to give the initial push, although, in the longer term, such a requirement would only be of use if the probationer himself really wanted to take advantage of the specialist help available to him.

Rather than an additional requirement being made by the court, some sheriffs thought the authority should be placed firmly in the hands of the social worker. One said that he always stressed this when placing an offender on probation:

I make it a condition of probation that they should do what they are told by their social worker. I say to them 'if your social worker tells you to attend this clinic or that clinic, or whatever the case may be, then you will do that'. I think it gives the social worker a bit more authority over the person on a day by day, week by week basis, than the court necessarily has once the order has been made.

When we interviewed sheriffs, a recent addition to sentencing options had been the introduction of the six month probation order, and we were keen to know what use was being made of this. In fact, only one sheriff had made such an order:

I can't remember the exact circumstances. It might have been a mother who had previous involvement with the social work department, or an offence involving a child. I thought 'well, all she needs is a little lift for the next six months'. but I welcomed it; it gives more flexibility to the whole thing.

Apart from this one positive comment, other sheriffs who had considered the matter, were all of the opinion that six months was really too short a period to accomplish anything very useful, given the present pattern of supervision:

I have conditioned myself to a year or 18 months. It seems to me that not a lot could be done within six months, particularly if manpower problems prevent regular supervision. The six month period would have to be a different type of probation from what goes on now.

One or two sheriffs knew very little about it, but still held firm opinions. One declared:

Well, I've no doubt I've read about that. I read all these things that come in, but it didn't register, and it's obviously something I haven't taken aboard. Thinking of it now, I can't see how six months probation could be of any use to anybody.

7.3 Conclusions relating to recommendations

7.3.1 Sheriffs' views on the key to expansion

As we have seen, the two main factors inhibiting sheriffs from making more probation disposals are lack of recommendations from social workers, and doubt about the adequacy of probation supervision. It is evident that sheriffs are often surprised by the lack of a recommendation for probation, when it appears to be a suitable option. Since there is a general hesitancy to make an order unless a recommendation to that effect has been made, more recommendations backed up by sound reasoning and stating how probation might be used would be welcomed by sheriffs.

As far as lack of confidence in social work supervision is concerned, lack of knowledge about the supervisory process, lack of feedback, general impressions and hearsay about delays in allocation, and lack of reporting back and breaching when things go wrong, all seem to be contributory factors. One way of providing more consistent feedback would be the introduction of completion reports. The majority of sheriffs welcomed this idea and identified a number of potential benefits. A number of sheriffs would also welcome a greater degree of specialisation within the present generic structure, feeling that, in general, social workers are not as down to earth as specialist probation officers.

7.3.2 Obstacles to well reasoned and purposeful recommendations

Even where guidelines exist, social workers differ in their interpretation of official policy, and there is considerable variation in less formal guidance from office to office, and even between different teams in the same office. Some workers believe that no recommendation should be made, others that only the suitability, or otherwise, of probation should be included. Many experienced workers, with good court links, have no hesitancy in making broader based recommendations, including the possible use of a custodial sentence.

Even workers who think they should not do so, frequently make recommendations to meet what they see as the expectations of court and colleagues. In fact, sheriffs, like social workers, have widely differing views. In general there is little opposition to recommendations being made, although there are differences of opinion about their necessity, the way they should be made, what they should cover, and the influence they have on the sentencing process.

Recommendations by social workers are influenced by their perception of the suitability of an offender for probation, their background experience, and whether they start from a court or welfare based approach to supervision.

Additionally however, organisational and individual workload management factors are sometimes a determining influence, with social workers either trying to control their workload by not recommending probation even when it would appear to be an appropriate disposal, or on the other hand, making a recommendation in an effort to ensure that the case is allocated and obtains a fair share of scant resources.

7.3.3 The suitability of offender rather than offence types

There does not seem to be a any one clear view among either sheriffs, social workers or probationers themselves about the suitability of any particular offender group for probation, although first offenders and long term 'last chancers' were mentioned most frequently. A number of sheriffs also mentioned women, although this seems to relate to the problems and consequences of other disposals, such as the care of children when a custodial sentence is given, rather than the inherent suitability of women for probation. In the main, probation is considered appropriate for a certain kind of person, rather than being related to the nature of the offence or any particular stage of the criminal career.

The motivation of the offender is of crucial importance, as is the identification of some kind of problem or situation which is related to the offending behaviour, and which is potentially amenable to social work help. From the point of view of sheriffs, the kind of person they consider suitable for probation is also influenced by the type of supervision they think the offender is likely to receive. This is seen as essentially welfare rather than court based, and may suggest a sentencing policy which helps to explain the fact that none of the probationers in the sample were 'professional' criminals.

7.4 Conclusions relating to the supervision of probation orders

7.4.1 Differences in allocation procedures

In chapter 4, we looked at the different methods by which cases were allocated. Social workers prefer either direct allocation by a senior social worker, who knows and takes account of the worker's special interests or areas of expertise, or allocation meetings where there is room for discussion and negotiation, with the senior making the final decisions. Both methods allow for a degree of individual specialisation and skill development, within a team which can build up a pool of shared knowledge and expertise. In this way worker satisfaction and client service are both enhanced.

7.4.2 Existence and knowledge of practice guidelines

Knowledge of guidelines, even where they exist, is extremely variable; from office to office, team to team, and between workers in the same team. The extent to which they are absorbed and implemented depends, not only on their existence and availability, but on more individual factors such as the worker's interest in probation, the availability of in-service training and, most importantly, the senior's attitude in encouraging and supporting this area of work.

7.4.3 The low priority of probation

At an organisational level, social workers place probation about half way down a nominal scale, lower than all forms of work with children, but higher than non-statutory areas of work such as the elderly or mentally handicapped. There is a widespread feeling that service to probationers falls short of what is required because of other priorities. Cases are sometimes unallocated, occasionally for considerable periods, and social workers complained of insufficient time to attend court or supervise probationers effectively. At an individual level, the priority given to individual probation cases appears to depend very much on the perceived welfare needs of the case rather than its probation requirements.

7.4.5 Very few probationers receive a satisfactory level of service.

Using the basic four point level of service measure, it is immediately striking how few probationers receive a satisfactory standard of service. Nearly half of all the cases examined were categorised as receiving a 'poor' or 'very poor' service. Within this generally gloomy picture there are, however, considerable variations. In general, the level of service is considerably higher in the smaller court areas, and within the area covered by the large city court, cases with a reasonable or satisfactory level of service tend to be found in the less pressurised and more suburban areas on the edge of the city. From our limited data, it appears that the chances of a probation case receiving an adequate level of service in the inner city are slim.

7.5 Conclusions relating to evaluating probation

7.5.1 Identifying effective probation supervisors

From our examination of social workers' practice and probationer responses we conclude that there are certain features which make for 'suitable' supervisors who are likely to offer sound probation supervision. An interest in probation and work with offenders is paramount, as is the opportunity to develop this interest and acquire the skills and expertise which lead to confident and competent practice in working with the courts as well as probationers.

From the probationers' point of view the social worker's attitude is as important as the content of help offered, and a number of helpful attitudes on the part of supervising social workers were identified. These, perhaps surprisingly, focus more on the court based 'control' aspect of probation than on the 'welfare' strand. The ability of the social worker to carry authority easily, showing firmness and control in a relaxed way, and not let the probationer get away with things is important, as is the ability to confront the probationer in a straightforward way.

'Pushy' social workers, who consistently demand real effort and change, are seen as showing genuine interest and concern, helping to create and maintain the motivation of the probationer. This is particularly important with adult recidivists, although in general 'persistent offenders need persistent social workers'. Although there was less concordance about unhelpful attitudes, there were complaints about social workers who were rushed, judgmental, domineering, hypocritical and insufficiently strict.

From the cases examined, specialist probation rather than generic initial training does not, in itself, seem to lead to 'better' supervision. Certainly the probation trained workers we came across did offer a good level and quality of service, as did an unqualified worker with long term interest and experience in probation. So, however, did interested and experienced generic workers, Probation trained social workers tended to make more use the court based befriending approach than did other social workers.

7.5.2 Sheriffs' varied measures of probation 'success'

There is no clear single view from sheriffs as to what constitutes a successful probation order. Some said they find it difficult to answer this question in view of the lack of clarity about the aims and objectives social workers have in mind, and the lack of consistent feedback about the way probation supervision is carried out. The majority of sheriffs however, do not, as we initially expected, measure success solely by the fact that no further offences have been committed during the course of an order, and are of the opinion that other criteria also need to be considered. These include: less frequency in offending, signs of increased responsibility, evidence that the probationer is making positive use of social work guidance and advice, and the general degree of improvement shown by the probationer.

7.6 Conclusions relating to improving probation.

7.6.1 One-to-one supervision as the dominant and static mode of service

As detailed earlier in the chapter, none of the probationers in our sample systematically received any other type of social work intervention than traditional one-to-one casework, although some attended other agencies for specific problems. Social workers were often angry and frustrated because of failed attempts to develop a wider range of more creative practice initiatives, which would better meet the needs of many probationers. There was no evidence in the sample of the use of systematic group work, special probation projects, or structured probation clinics, all of which can provide useful additions or alternatives to traditional one-to-one supervision. However, by the end of the research period one group had been started in the area of the study and there was certainly a keen awareness that such developments are badly needed before probation could be developed to its full potential.

7.6.2 Changes of social worker adversely affects probation

Changes of social worker, whether through promotion, transfer or resignation, frequently means that probation cases - not the highest priority in the first instance - not only face periods of unallocation, but are often allocated to inexperienced workers, with scant knowledge of probation legislation and no experience of working with the court, something about which they are often extremely nervous. Additionally, they have little or no knowledge of local networks and resources, an important factor in work with many offenders. We found that workers with a background in working with offenders, were particularly adept at knowing about and obtaining resources which might benefit their probationers. Lack of continuity in the supervision of probationers, for whatever reason, at best does little for their progress, and at worst results in inadequate and often inappropriate social work intervention.

7.6.3 Some specialisation in probation supervision might improve matters

There does seem to be a general idea that all social workers in area offices can and should be able to do a bit of everything. In reality this sometimes means that social workers carry probation cases in which they are not really interested and for which their skills are inadequate, and also that they skimp on the work they like least. In offices where there is, or recently has been, some degree of specialist organisation, such as a court team, for example, workers are generally more comfortable with the statutory aspects of probation work and use these more constructively in their work with probationers.

Since the completion of the research, national standards on work with offenders have been issued by the Scottish Office and are in the process of being implemented throughout Scotland. Many of the ideas and suggestions given to us by the various participants in the probation process and presented in this book, were one of the sources of data used to inform the discussion about and preparation of these standards.

It may be that the introduction of national standards, together with the appointment of specialist workers and managers, now under way in some districts, will help to stimulate greater interest in work with offenders generally, and, in particular, aid the development of knowledge, expertise and confidence in working with the courts and probationers, to maximise the opportunities provided by 'the conditional suspension of punishment'.

Bibliography

Bottoms, A.E. and McWilliams, W. (1979), 'A Non Treatment Paradigm for Probation Practice', *British Journal of Social Work*, 9, pp. 159-202.

Celnick, A. (1985), 'From Paradigm to Practice in a Special Probation Project', *British Journal of Social Work*, 15, pp. 223-41.

Coker, J.B. (1982), 'Sentenced to Social Work? - An Experiment in Probation Practice in Hampshire (England)', *International Journal of Offender Therapy and Comparative Criminology*, 26, pp. 27-31.

Davies, M. (1969), *Probationers in their Social Environment*, HMSO, London.

Davies, M. and Sinclair, I. (1971), 'Families, Hostels and Delinquents', *British Journal of Criminology*, 11, pp. 213-229.

Davies, M. (1973), *An Index of Social Environment*, HMSO, London.

Davies, M. (1974), 'The Assessment of Environment in Social Work Research', *Social Casework* January, pp. 3-12.

Davies, M. (1979), 'Through the Eyes of the Probationer', *Probation Journal*, 26, pp. 84-9.

Davies, M. (1981), *The Essential Social Worker*, Heinemann, London.

Emery, F.E. and Trist, E.L. (1969), 'The Causal Texture of Organisational Environments' in Emery, E.L. (ed.), *Systems Thinking*, Penguin, London.

Fielding, N. (1986), *Probation Practice - Client Support under Social Control*, Gower, Aldershot.

Hardiker, P. (1977), 'Social Work Ideologies in the Probation Service', *British Journal of Social Work*, 7, pp. 131-53.

Hardiker, P. and Webb, D. (1979), 'Explaining Deviant Behaviour: The Social Context of "Action" and "Infraction" Accounts in the Probation Service', *Sociology*, 13, pp. 1-17.

Hil, R. (1982), 'Conceptual Images of Social Work and Probation Practice: A Case Study', *International Journal of Offender Therapy and Comparative Criminology*, pp. 255-64.

109

HMSO, (1988), *Punishment, Custody and the Community*, HMSO, London.

HOWARD LEAGUE (1976), *Probation in Scotland*, Howard League, London.

Lawson, C. (1978), *The Probation Officer as Prosecutor*, Institute of Criminology, Cambridge.

Monger, M. (1972), *Casework in Probation*, Butterworth, London.

Moore, G. and Wood, C. (1981), *Social Work and Criminal Law in Scotland*, Aberdeen University Press, Aberdeen.

Parker, H. (1974), *A View from the Boys*, David and Charles, London.

Parsloe, P. (1967), *The Work of the Probation and After-Care Officer*, Routledge and Kegan Paul, London.

Sainsbury, E., *et al.*, (1982), *Social Work in Focus*, Routledge and Kegan Paul, London.

SCOTTISH OFFICE, (1982), *Social Enquiry Reports in Scotland*, HMSO, Edinburgh.

Titmuss, R. (1954), 'The Administrative Setting of Social Service', *Case Conferenece*, 1.

UNITED NATIONS, (1951), *Probation and Related Measures*, UN Publications, New York.